HOUSES
OF GOD

Dedication

For my uncle, The Reverend Andrew Nicolicchia, O.P.

HOUSES
OF GOD

Religious Architecture for a New Millennium

MICHAEL J. CROSBIE

images
Publishing

Published in Australia in 2006 by
The Images Publishing Group Pty Ltd
ABN 89 059 734 431
6 Bastow Place, Mulgrave, Victoria 3170, Australia
Tel: +61 3 9561 5544 Fax: +61 3 9561 4860
books@images.com.au
www.imagespublishing.com

National Library of Australia Cataloguing-in-Publication entry:

Crosbie, Michael J. (Michael James).
Houses of God: religious architecture for a new millennium.

ISBN 1 920744 97 5 (v. III).

1. Church buildings – Pictorial works.
2. Church architecture – Pictorial works. I. Architecture for the Gods.

726.5

Edited by Aisha Hasanovic

Designed by The Graphic Image Studio Pty Ltd, Australia
www.tgis.com.au

Digital production by Splitting Image Colour Studio Pty Ltd

Printed by Sing Cheong Printing Co. Ltd. Hong Kong

Included on www.imagespublishing.com is a page for news and
updates to the information contained in IMAGES' books. It may
contain updated information regarding this book.

Contents

Contents continued

Introduction

What makes a place sacred?

Creating a place to meet the divine must be one of the most ambitious yet hope-laden of human activities. Stone is put upon stone to create an environment, the success of which ultimately cannot be measured. How do we know if we have produced a sacred space? Is the space itself sacred, or is it merely a container for sacred acts? Can the faithful not meet the celestial in places that are poorly designed, meagerly constructed, and less than works of art? Of course they can. But it is a designer's hope and faith (and the purpose of this book to document) that architecture can provide an immeasurable dimension to religious experience.

Experiences of beauty that move one to tears enter our hearts via the same portal through which God is made known to us. Architecture, music, poetry, painting, sculpture—all these arts are present in the making of the best sacred spaces, as aids to prayer and worship. Rather than distractions on our journey to meet the divine, they can help prepare us for the trip. Light, color, sacred music, the lyrical quality of prayer—all these esthetic experiences join with the artful molding of form and space to help open within us channels to the divine.

How do we define these holy places, these epicenters of belief? We know such spaces when we experience them. Most of these buildings occupy a central place in a neighborhood, town, or city. We have no trouble recognizing a church, a synagogue, a temple, or a mosque. From the grandest to the most humble, houses of worship have certain physical characteristics that appeal to all our senses, our heart, and our intellect. Outside, their materials are often precious and placed with care, covered with carvings that have symbolic and allegorical value. Through their embellishment and adornment, they tell us stories. These buildings are "books" that can be "read," recounting articles of faith. Beautiful stained glass windows can lift us from our earthly concerns and raise our spirits to an ethereal realm. We move our fingers along stone, tile, wrought-iron, and carved wood to sense their permanence.

Large expansive spaces are often found inside these sacred buildings. Vast interiors not only accommodate those who come to pray, but are symbolically big enough for God to join us there. A soft glow falls from above, filters through the sanctuary, and occupies the space with us. Shafts of sunlight spill from upper windows to the cool stone floors below, evanescent ladders to the heavens. The sounds of footsteps, whispered prayers, and hymns echo within these sacred chambers, amplifying our presence before the divine. Flickering candles of beeswax and trails of incense fill our noses with uncommon scents from another time and place.

This is what our religious buildings are made of—a totaling of their physical reality. But what is the magic ingredient that makes these places sacred, that sets them apart as realms between heaven and earth?

Such spaces cannot be made sacred merely through their physical qualities—walls, floors, and ceilings. This material setting makes possible the sanctification of a place only through us: a gathering of souls in the act of celebrating liturgy or praying quietly at our lives' most spiritually challenging times. One manifestation is wear. Frederick Evans's famous photo of the Sea of Steps in Wells Cathedral in England (above) perfectly captures this facet of the sacred in its river of worn stairs, which show the cumulative wear of pilgrims through the centuries. When we tread upon these worn stones, we follow the path of believers before us. The groove they have made is a strait through which flows a community of faith, a family of believers that we connect to through the building. The sacred place embodies the substantiation of faith.

But a sacred place is more than just worn steps. It is the place where we are welcomed into the community, where bonds are forged with others, where we bid final farewells to fellow believers, a place that takes on the patina of life and faith. It can be a place where life-changing events have occurred, where ultimate sacrifices were made. This is why even secular places can be sacred. Think of the cemetery at Gettysburg where rest, as Lincoln said during its dedication, those who "gave the last full measure of devotion." Lincoln knew that we cannot make a sacred place simply by building one and declaring it so. Of Gettysburg, he observed: "… we cannot dedicate, we cannot consecrate, we cannot hallow this ground." Gettysburg is sacred because of the people who died there, and what they died for. In the same way, many people now see the World Trade Center site as a sacred place. Through such environments, we become part of something mysterious and much larger than ourselves.

The projects in this book comprise an overview of contemporary settings for worship through which people enter a community of faith. Many denominations are represented in these buildings: Catholic, Protestant, Buddhist, and Jewish traditions and sects. Some restate the patterns of sacred architecture seen for hundreds of years, such as the design of the Perpetual Adoration Chapel at Holy Trinity Church, modeled on ancient country churches, eg, St. Etienne in Vignory, France. The chapel includes century-old Bavarian stained glass windows. Another example is the First Parish Congregational Church in Saco, Maine (1, next page), which replaces a church that burned to the ground. This design responds to the fact that the site is in an historic district: it links the new structure to the building traditions of New England Congregational Churches, yet its arrangement of inside spaces meets the contemporary needs of the congregation.

An even older architectural precedent is evident in several sacred spaces possessing the stark purity and hallowed austerity of early Cistercian churches from nearly a millennium ago. Tadao Ando's Church of the Light, completed a number of years ago, is included here as a modern wellspring of ascetic sacred space. Ando's more recent Komyo-Ji Temple in Saijo, Japan (2), does in wood what the Church of the Light accomplishes in concrete.

The Holy Rosary Catholic Oratory in Louisiana comes the closest, I believe, to the Cistercian ideal of a sacred emptiness into which we pour ourselves. Through natural light and unfinished concrete alone, this space—a virtual sensory-deprivation chamber—invites meditation and spiritual reflection.

Another sacred space with roots in the Cistercian tradition is the Kirche auf der Platte in Vienna (3), a simple cube of space articulated at its corners to form a Greek Cross in plan. The single-material exterior of black stainless steel contrasts with an interior of beechwood. This enclosure is punctured with a scattering of porthole windows, allowing points of sunlight to flood the space and move about it like circular spirits over the course of the day.

This collection of religious buildings includes a number of very grand sacred spaces, such as the new Cathedral of our Lady of Guadalupe, the restoration of and additions to Sacred Heart Cathedral, and the Padre Pio Pilgrimage Church in San Giovanni Rotondo, Italy (4). But there are several very small sacred spaces that possess the same power to move us to contemplation. Grace Chapel at St. Mark's Episcopal Church in Austin, Texas (5), uses indigenous stone, wood, and glass to inspire awe on a modest scale. Though tiny, the chapel has become a neighborhood landmark.

The East End Temple occupies the interior of a former Richard Morris Hunt house in New York City. A narrow passage leads from the entry to a sanctuary that is meager in square footage but marvelous in its height, accentuated by a cascade of sunlight from above the ark. Maya Lin's Riggo-Lynch Chapel has a small interior that has the ability to expand into the surrounding Tennessee landscape. In a clinic in New Orleans, the diminutive, nondenominational Kate and Laurence Eustis Chapel (6) is realized in woven layers of wood, contrasting with glass, and the soothing sound of running water. On a wooded site in Minnesota, the House of Prayer Oratory, at only 1000 square feet, contains a circular space lined with birch paneling. The ceiling opens like the petals of a flower above one's head to welcome the spirit, or suggests the chambers of a heart in which the Almighty might reside.

Each of these small projects provides a certain antidote—a potent tonic of sanity—to the profusion of megachurches that have sprung up like weeds across America and in other parts of the world. Perhaps we are beginning to see a new trend in the design of sacred space that reaffirms the value of intimate scale in our relationship with a living God.

Ultimately, every House of God is a home for us too. Congregations and clergy strive to make a place to meet the divine with family members present and past. The better church architects listen as carefully as they would to a family's dream of a new home, dedicated to every new life in the spirit, and the lives of those who have gone before. The Antioch

Baptist Church in Perry County, Alabama, designed and built by Auburn
University's Rural Studio, makes incarnate this power of sacred space.
Built mostly of materials recycled from Antioch's previous, century-old
rural church, the new building orients the pews along a glass wall and
across an implied aisle from the final resting place in the churchyard
of deceased congregation members. During worship, church family
members, living and dead, are united across time and space, home again.

Michael J. Crosbie

1

2

5

3

4

6

PROJECTS

Kirche auf der Platte

Heinz Tesar

This church belongs within the tradition of 'sacred building on the square' and is the prelude to the Donau City section of Vienna—a modern residential and business center. The new church reacts in specific ways to the context. It is slightly turned toward east, off center from the main diagonal formed by the main street of Donau City. This shift creates (with the bank building across the street) a small square.

The massing of the church is calibrated to the urban space it occupies, reflecting the importance of this square in the city. In contrast to the larger buildings around it, the church is a compact, precise monument that stands out as a landmark.

The four corners of the square plan are chamfered at different heights to imply a Greek cross. The resulting eight outside edges around the church's periphery symbolize the creation, Christ's resurrection, and his second coming on the eighth day. The sunken outdoor garden in front of the pastoral rooms on the lower level emphasizes the anchoring of the building to the ground, the rootedness of the church to the site.

The cladding is of black stainless steel panels with deep 'drilled' holes that suggest the building's weight. The reflection of light off the panels, the holes, and the glass make the façade a living hull, a skin. Through its openings shines onto the square the light of the sacred space inside, and vice versa.

Inside, the sanctuary is lined with light beech paneling. The sinuous roof opening suggests the chest wound of Christ on the cross. Depending on the time of the day and season, the sun creates ever-changing patterns in the space, which encompasses and embraces the visitor and offers a protected sanctum, without being entirely off from the outside world.

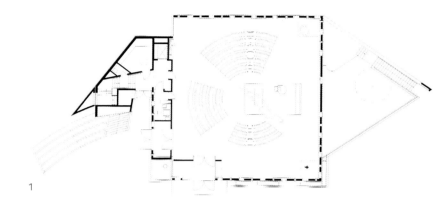

1

2

1 Sanctuary level plan
2 Roof top with "wound" skylight
3 Light reflected on stainless steel skin

3

Opposite
Detail of black stainless steel cladding

5 *Interior's restrained material pallet*

5

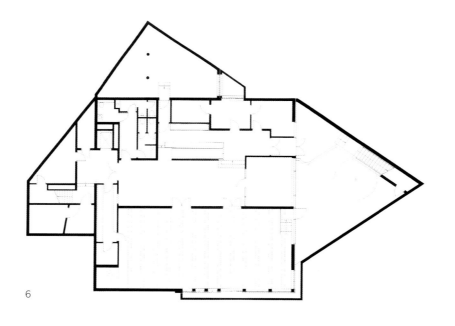

6

7

8

Photography: Christian Richters

9

Temple Bat Yahm Torah Center

Lehrer Architects

The Temple Bat Yahm Torah Center is a spiritual campus of buildings and landscapes, bathed in light, located in the temperate coastal climate of Newport Beach, California, within a mile of the Pacific Ocean. Its mission is summed up in the image of Jacob's Ladder, embodied in the diaphanous pavilion/baldachino floating in the chapel. The Center is rooted in the ground, in the daily activity of an engaged community.

The design reflects the Rabbi's words and mandate to create buildings and landscapes that are grounded in this world, the horizontal realm, "where God's immanence is felt," and that engage the heavens, the vertical realm, where "God's transcendence is embodied." Light is the medium that binds these realms, expressing the Rabbi's belief that light and spirit are synonymous.

The design improvements transform an existing facility from a virtually windowless, single building into an ensemble of spaces that form a spiritual enclave. The 5.3-acre campus of new and old buildings, new landscapes and public spaces comprise the new Center. Emblematic and iconic places, processions, forms, and spaces house this spiritual community. Processional axes are explicitly defined places of architecture and landscape. Several patterns and paths cross the terrain. Color emphasizes the themes of the campus.

Sustainability strategies featured in this project include carefully controlled daylighting, natural ventilation, highly efficient mechanical ventilation, watershed management (water retention and detention) and permeable surfaces, native planting, and maximized outdoor circulation.

Parking, particularly in places like Orange County, often drives the site design. The Center's "parking park," for both parking and play, provides a lawn with tandem parking stalls to allow the area to be used as a lawn and park the majority of the year, and as a parking lot when needed. This green parking solution virtually doubles the perceived size of the campus, setting the buildings in the middle of the park landscape, as opposed to at the edge of a large asphalt lot.

1

1   Campus of sacred buildings and structures
2   "Parking park" uses grass instead of asphalt
3   Pathways link buildings across the site

2

3

4

5

6

7

4 Connection between sanctuary and sky
5 Sky opening follows curve of seating
6 Light from above and views to outdoors
7 Lantern over sanctuary recalls Jacob's Ladder
8 Colors are balanced with light
9 Natural light is abundant in classrooms

Photography: courtesy Marvin Rand

8

9

First Parish Congregational Church

Donham & Sweeney Architects

The new First Parish Congregational Church in Saco, Maine, replaces a 137-year-old building that burned to the ground in 2000. The congregation members' three-year "exile" to a nearby school opened their minds to new possibilities. Early on, they realized that the space needs and form of worship and fellowship appropriate for 1863 were not the same as for today. They also recognized that what many enjoyed most in their weekly gatherings was the experience of fellowship and community.

These needs led directly to the basic organization of the building, with both main entrances leading to the central atrium, with the fellowship hall placed at one end of the atrium and the sanctuary at the other. Seating in the sanctuary is arranged in a gentle curve so that worshippers can see each other, which helps to foster a sense of community. The upper level holds a balcony and projection booth for the sanctuary as well as church offices and a meeting space. The lower level, sunk halfway into the ground, contains all the Christian education rooms plus choir spaces.

Expectations were that the new building would have a landmark quality similar to the former building. The site is in an historic district, subject to the review such districts entail. First Parish is a large building for a New England Protestant church, but at 32,000 square feet, only 20 percent is devoted to the sanctuary. To address all these issues, the building is broken into three primary forms with the most important, the sanctuary, being the biggest and located facing the main commercial thoroughfare. The atrium gathering space and the fellowship hall read as separate forms, with all three supported on the foundation of Christian education.

Vertical board-and-batten siding, a Maine tradition going back 150 years, provides a visible verticality. Large windows in the sanctuary and fellowship hall connect the life of the church to the outside world and vice versa. A consistent vocabulary of detailing unites the various interior spaces with the exterior of the building.

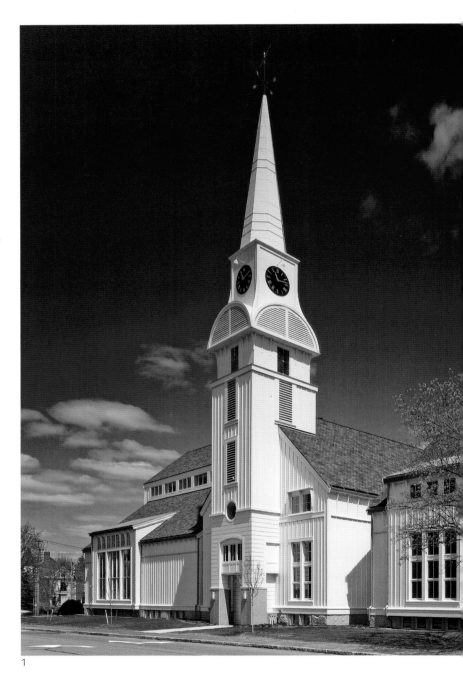

1

2

3 *Upper level plan*

4 *Ground level entry plan*

5 *Sanctuary with barrel vault roof*

6 *Entry to narthex from atrium*

7 *View from altar area toward narthex*

Photography: Bruce T. Martin

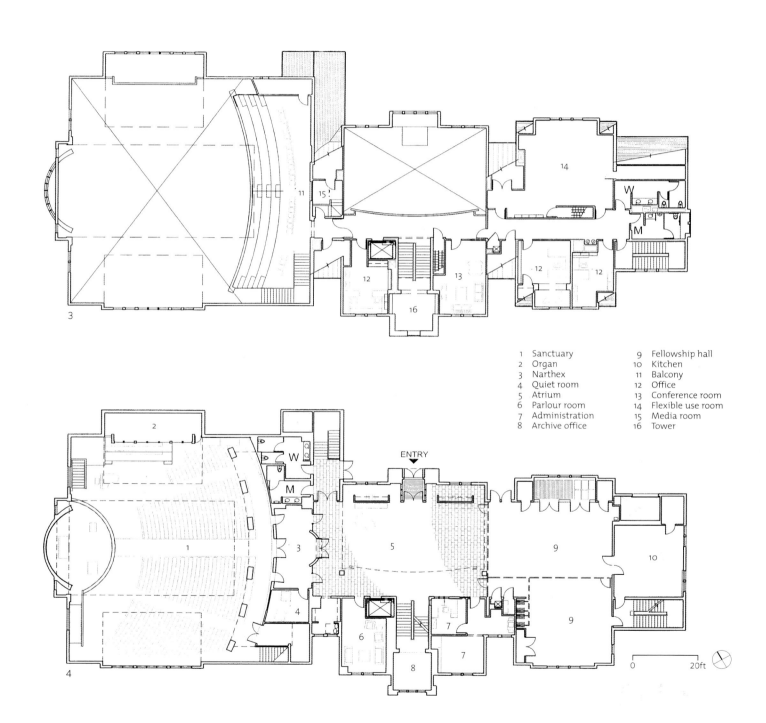

1	Sanctuary	9	Fellowship hall
2	Organ	10	Kitchen
3	Narthex	11	Balcony
4	Quiet room	12	Office
5	Atrium	13	Conference room
6	Parlour room	14	Flexible use room
7	Administration	15	Media room
8	Archive office	16	Tower

5

6

7

St. Mark's Cathedral Expansion

Olson Sundberg Kundig Allen Architects

St. Mark's Cathedral's vast interior volume is a powerfully spiritual space—unpretentious yet majestic. Never completed as planned due to the Depression, and renovated several times over the nearly 70 years of its existence, the cathedral nevertheless possesses great dignity and presence, and is much loved by the spiritual and secular communities of Seattle, Washington.

The expansion and renovations enhance and enlarge upon the spiritual qualities inherent in the building, while improving liturgical and functional elements. As part of the expansion and remodeling, the "temporary" concrete walls of the west façade were covered with Indiana limestone, completing the exterior as originally intended and putting a stop to the years of deterioration through water penetration. The remainder of the exterior will be clad in later phases.

A new 21-foot-diameter window is part of the new west wall, designed to limit direct western light. The large window's design is based on a Celtic Cross. The central glass area is clear to create a focal point of light into the Cathedral's interior.

A glass and steel reredos on the west wall further modulates the western light. The reredos extends 57-feet from floor to ceiling, with space for a small chapel behind it. The reredos is a combination of laminated and kiln-fused glass in two primary elements, a monochromatic grid of glass panels, and a 28-foot-diameter glass "rose." Surrounding the rose are 200 one-inch-thick, kiln-fused panels. Seen together, the reredos and large window form a three-dimensional, contemporary sculptural interpretation of a traditional rose window. Standing at the entrance to the nave, these two elements, reredos and large window, become a single element.

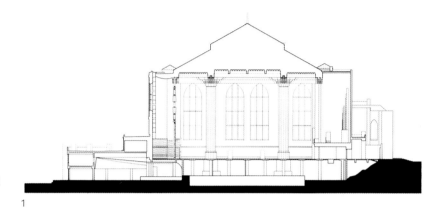

1

2

1 *West–east section through sanctuary*
2 *Cathedral as it overlooks the city*
3 *West wall with new window and cladding*

3

4 *Reredos window and wall*
5 *Reredos window recalls a rose*
6 *Sanctuary level plan*

4

5

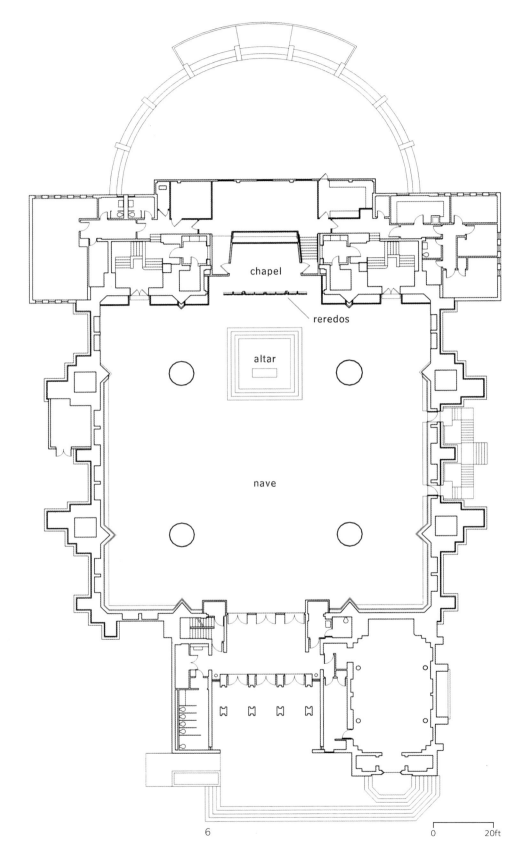

chapel

reredos

altar

nave

6

0   20ft

7   Behind reredos is new round window

8   Sanctuary's west wall with reredos on axis

Photography: Tim Bies; Eduardo Calderon;
    Ed Carpenter; Olson Sundberg Kundig Allen Architects

Unity Spiritual Center

Blunden Barclay and Associates, Architects

The goal of this project was to renovate an existing worship center in Westlake, Ohio, to create an intimate and spiritual sanctuary that would support worship and meditation. This was to be done for a construction cost of only $65,000. The budget constraints meant that each potential change had to be thoroughly evaluated for its cost and relevant contribution to the overall character of the space.

Two major decisions were to change the orientation of the space 90 degrees (from the narrow end of the rectangular space to one of the longer side walls) and to use moveable chairs rather than pews. It was also decided to move the piano and organ from the altar podium to a place at the rear of the seating. These changes resulted in an intimacy that gives the congregation an increased awareness of each other, fostering a strong sense of shared worship and community. Using chairs rather than pews has the added benefit of allowing the space to be flexible.

A new platform and reredos were added with carefully integrated ramps for access to the platform. The reredos also functions as a screen for projection. New lighting and controls provide the ability to create varying moods with light in order to support different gatherings and programs. A new sound system and digital projection system add to the versatility of the space. The existing ceiling and lighting were left in place for budgetary reasons. These items can easily be replaced when funds become available.

The result is a transformation of the space to one of serenity and peace, creating a welcoming spiritual home for the congregation.

1   *New orientation and layout of worship space*
2   *Existing layout before renovation*
3   *Altar podium with reredos wall for projection*
4   *Ramp is discreetly incorporated into low wall*
5   *Movable seating allows flexibility*
6   *Pews in existing space before renovation*

Photography: Blunden Barclay and Associates, Architects

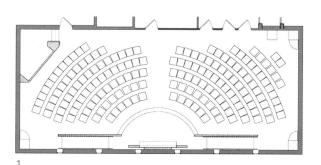

1

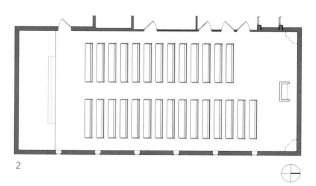

2

3

4

5

6

Church of the Light

Tadao Ando Architect & Associates

Tadao Ando's icon of modern church design is located on a tight, 8862-square-foot site in a quiet residential suburb of Osaka, Japan. It consists of a rectangular volume sliced through at a 15-degree angle by a completely freestanding wall that separates the entrance from the chapel. Light penetrates the profound darkness of this 1200-square-foot box through the void of a cross, which is cut into the altar wall. The floor and pews are made of rough wood scaffolding planks, which are low cost and also ultimately suited to the Spartan, pure character of the space.

Ando notes of this design that he has "always used natural materials for the parts of a building that come into contact with people's hands or feet, as I am convinced that materials having substance, such as wood or concrete, are invaluable for building, and that it is essentially through our senses that we become aware of architecture."

Openings are limited in this space, which intensifies the little light there is. The brilliance of the cross is experienced only against a backdrop of darkness. The linear pattern formed on the floor by rays from the sun and a migrating cross of light express with purity man's spiritual relationship with nature.

Nature's presence is also limited to the element of light and is rendered in an exceedingly abstract way. In responding to such an abstraction, Ando believes that the architecture grows continually purer.

1

1   *Altar wall exterior with cruciform window*

Opposite

   Interior is pierced by the light of the cross

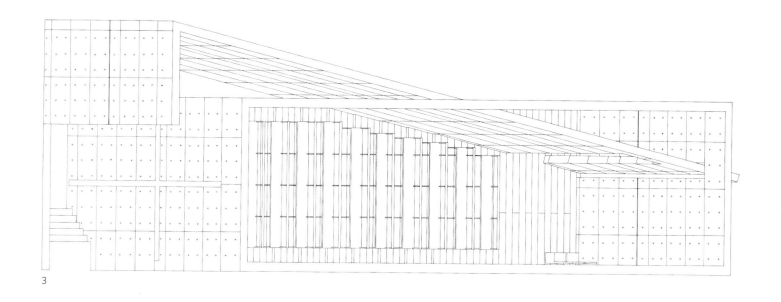

3

4

5

3 West–east section of church interior
4 Illuminated cross aligned with central aisle
5 Cross of light makes its journey through space
6 Section shows raked seating
7 Concrete's material texture remains exposed

Photography: Mitsuo Matsuoka

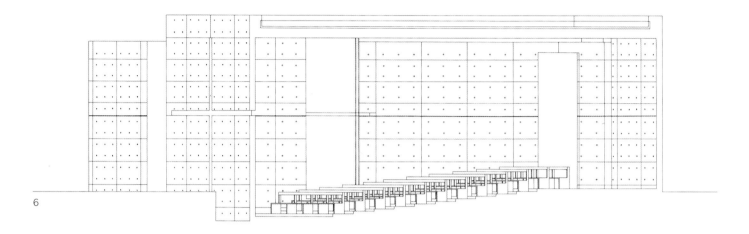

6

7

Cathedral of Our Lady of Guadalupe

RD Habiger & Associates

The Roman Catholic Diocese of Dodge City, Kansas, is a tapestry of small towns and farmsteads set in a landscape of gently rolling hills, circular irrigated fields, and tree-lined water courses. The diocese wanted the cathedral to provide a worship setting for 2400 households, combining two existing ethnic parishes within a limited budget. The worship space was to exemplify the liturgical principles of Vatican II, and to be a dignified, authentic, and meaningful testament to the people of faith.

The cathedral rises out of the land, establishing a landmark seen from miles around. The building opens its arms, embracing a central welcoming plaza. The bell tower brings people to the plaza both visually and aurally. A place for the Easter fire marks the spiritual center of this setting. Textured sidewalks, terracotta floor tile, and limestone floor slabs provide association with places ancient and sacred. Door handles duplicating plump grapes and headed wheat ready for harvest greet visitors as they move through ceremonial doors.

Significant form-givers for the cathedral are materials that express warmth, an architectural palette that reflects the regional building vernacular, the use of daylight as a major interior element and to visually lighten the structure, the use of sacred geometric proportions, and the application of a central plan to honor Vatican II renewed liturgy. These factors are blended together to craft the cathedral's spirit of place.

An octagonal plan derived from the golden section provides seating for 1450 surrounding an island sanctuary. The octagonal configuration orchestrates placement of overhead trusses, limestone piers, windows, seating, and liturgical furniture. The design solution was to celebrate rather than to hide structural details, combined with an authentic expression of materials. Three levels of windows, each with textured and colored glazing, allow sunlight to penetrate into the worship space without creating glare. The central windows are located 62 to 88 feet above the sanctuary and shape the distinctive cupola-lantern roof form seen from the exterior.

1

1   *Entry is framed by bell tower and baptistery*
2   *Cathedral as experienced from the plains*

2

3

4

5

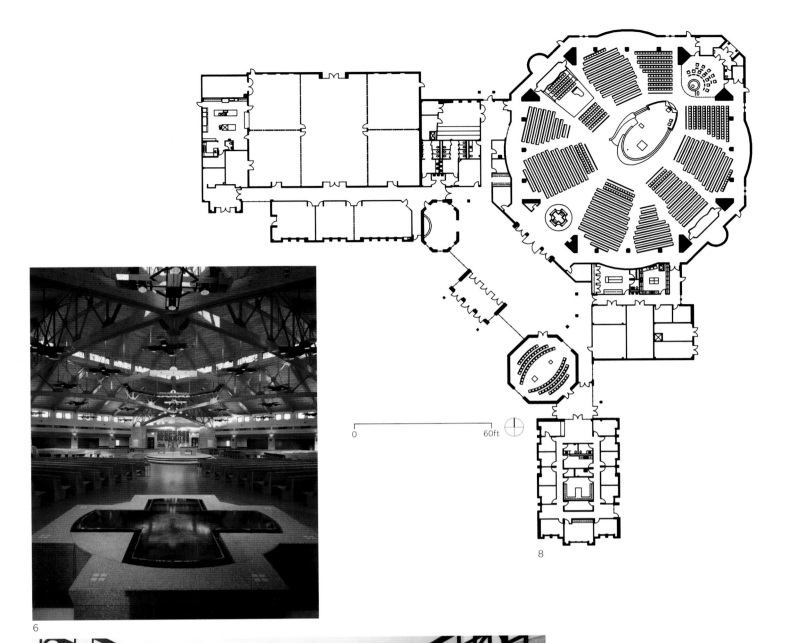

3 Doors from narthex to sanctuary
4 Wheat motif is used on door handles
5 Altar podium improves views for worship
6 Font at the sanctuary entrance
7 Chapel to Our Lady of Guadalupe
8 Sanctuary level plan

Photography: Robert Habiger; Rob McHenry

Congregation Beth Elohim

Finegold Alexander + Associates

This synagogue in Acton, Massachusetts, was originally built in 1978 as the first Jewish house of worship in this small New England community. The sanctuary of this compact structure also served as the synagogue's social hall.

In 1988, Finegold Alexander + Associates designed an addition to this small synagogue, which included a new worship space to the northeast, while the original sanctuary became a social hall.

The congregation, which began with fewer than 50 families, now numbers 350 families. The new addition is designed to accommodate 425 families.

The second addition brings the synagogue to nearly 24,000 square feet. It harmonizes with the original building, maintains the same sense of intimacy, and refines the function of the sanctuary. The new addition is a mirror in form of the plan that the architects developed in 1988. One enters through a new courtyard that joins the new and old buildings. The exterior is light-colored horizontal wood siding, which downplays the size of the expanded facility.

Just inside the entrance, a skylit community court leads on axis to the sanctuary, which is more than twice the size of the previous worship space. Overflow seating space for high holy days, found in the classroom wing to the northwest, doubles the capacity of the new sanctuary. The faceted ceilings slope up to an apex above the bema, while a central skylight fills the space with natural light.

The ark is a simple but statuesque free-standing structure with sandblasted glass doors inscribed with Hebrew text that is rendered as clear glass, providing an obscured view of the Torah scrolls inside.

1

2

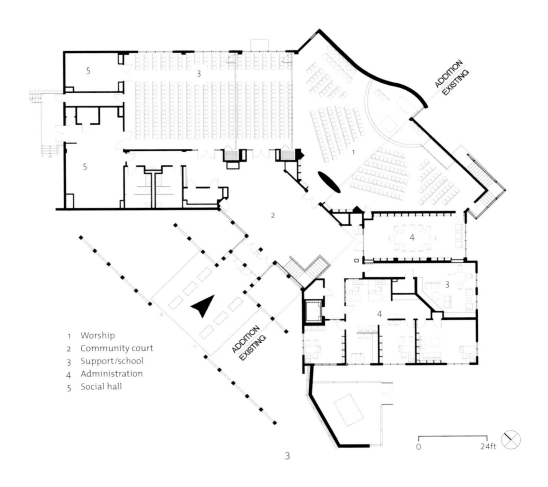

1 Worship
2 Community court
3 Support/school
4 Administration
5 Social hall

3

4

5

1 *Axial entry to expanded synagogue*

2 *Reception area leading to sanctuary*

3 *Sanctuary level plan*

4 *Sanctuary ceiling rises to apex*

5 *Ark with sandblasted glass*

Photography: Chris Johnson

St. Paul's Lutheran Church

RDG Planning and Design

This rural, Midwestern church community had been in existence as a congregation for more than 50 years.

It had outgrown its old building, which was beginning to fall into disrepair. The congregation decided to sell the current property and purchase land at the edge of the small town of Winterset, Iowa, and build a new church. The congregation's needs were modest: a worship space for 250 people, a fellowship/gathering space, a kitchen for extensive pot-luck dinners, and some offices and classrooms. A frugal construction budget called for flexible worship and fellowship space that could both expand as needed, a 24-hour chapel that could be used by those in need of sanctuary, modest materials and finishes, and simple forms that fit the rural context.

The landscape is composed of gradual rolling hills carpeted with various textures of grain and grass. Within this landscape are scattered farmsteads. These simple structures for storage and living stand squarely on the earth and form layered masses when viewed from varying angles across the fields. They are bold transitions between earth and sky.

The church's forms are simple masses layered with varying textures and patterns of materials much like Midwestern granary structures. The building can be seen as another farm structure on the edge of town forming a northwest anchor for the community. The building is layered, textured, and transparent in the evening when the glow and warmth of the interior spills out like the light of an Iowa barn.

Detailing is simple and modest. The large curved pivot doors on the interior are made of stick pieces of steel and wood with common steel wheels and hardware. The roof structure and tower have the atmosphere of rural farm structures. The large cross is made of natural Corten steel and forms the downspout for the chapel tower roof. Other materials on the exterior of the building are intended to remain natural and weather with time like the agrarian structures dotting the landscape.

1

1   *Interior of tower structure*

Opposite

   Tower suggests an agrarian structure

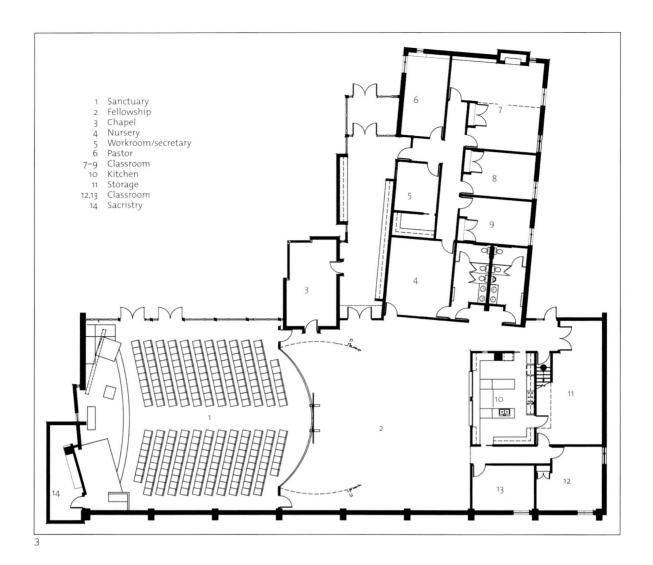

1 Sanctuary
2 Fellowship
3 Chapel
4 Nursery
5 Workroom/secretary
6 Pastor
7–9 Classroom
10 Kitchen
11 Storage
12,13 Classroom
14 Sacristy

3

3 *Worship level plan*
4 *Exterior suggests farming context*
5 *Entry side's welcoming gesture*
6 *Worship area open to fellowship space*
7 *Movable walls partition worship space*

Photography: Farshid Assassi

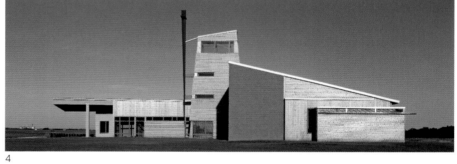

4

5

6

7

St. Martha Catholic Church

Eskew+Dumez+Ripple

This new Roman Catholic church, located in the middle of a suburban neighborhood in Harvey, Louisiana, is surrounded by the backyards of adjacent single-family houses. The worship space is strategically located at the center of the church property next to a large grove of trees, engaging the existing landscape. Plans envision this tree grove as an expanded worship space with a meditation walk containing an outdoor Stations of the Cross.

The church was designed through a series of interactive, hands-on workshops with the entire church congregation. More than 150 parishioners participated in six workshops over a four-month period. These workshops resulted in the final worship configuration and allowed all participants to provide significant input to the ultimate building design.

A layered plan relates the church front (neighborhood approach) to the everyday in contrast to the back (nature/repose), which is rendered as hallowed. The materials reinforce this duality: brick denotes gathering spaces at the church entry, which ties the building to its earthly, physical site. Alternately, metal panel cladding for the worship space presents a lighter, more ephemeral material. The campanile weaves both materials together in a symbolic knitting of sacred and secular to assert visually the church's public presence in the landscape.

The campanile is internally expressive, with tall vertical windows allowing natural light to fill the high volume of the day chapel within the tower's base. The soaring interior gives the chapel a dramatic spaciousness in contrast to the more intimately scaled main sanctuary.

A unique feature of the design is a result of a need to provide storm-water retention on site during heavy rainfalls. The inverted roof collects the rainwater, sloping to a single location where an over-scaled scupper drops water into a collection pond. This event takes place directly behind the altar, framed by a large window that allows worshippers to experience this intimate connection between sky and earth, thus reinforcing the position of the congregation and the church within a larger order.

1

2

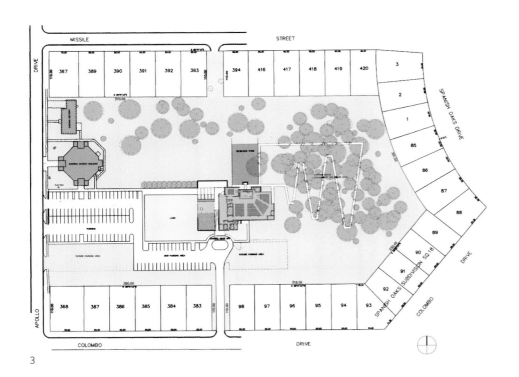

3

1 Open corner permits worship space views
2 Entry porch with glazed gathering area
3 Site plan
4 Church in its grove setting

4

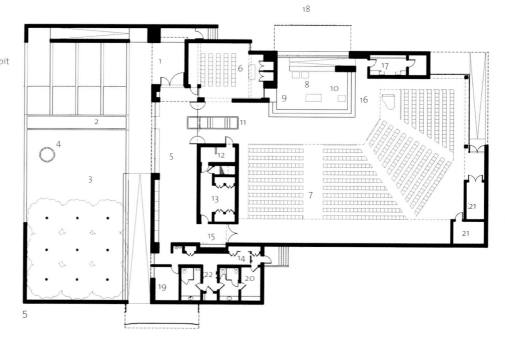

1 Entry porch
2 Reflecting pool
3 Gathering court
4 Ceremonial burning pit
5 Gathering space
6 Day chapel
7 Worship space
8 Altar
9 Tabernacle
10 Ambo
11 Baptismal font
12 Reconciliation room
13 Vestong area
14 Ushers' storage
15 Candle grotto
16 Music area
17 Work sacristy
18 Retention pond
19 Choir director's office
20 Bride's room
21 Storage
22 Restrooms

5

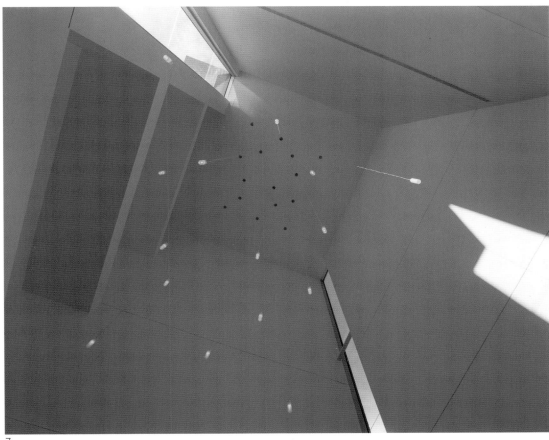

7

5 *Sanctuary level plan*
6 *Font bridges gathering*
   space and sanctuary
7 *Soaring space of tower*
8 *Sanctuary offers exterior views*

8

9 Seating gathered around altar

Photography: Timothy Hursley

9

McLean Bible Church

RNL, with Grimm & Parker Architects and LEO A DALY

Accommodating growth is an issue that has affected McLean Bible Church's planning and construction plans. After it purchased an existing 230,000-square-foot National Wildlife Federation building and 53 acres of land in McLean, Virginia, the church immediately commenced work on a two-phased project to remodel and expand the existing building. Phase I included a 1150-seat auditorium, classrooms, several large community rooms, and an 1100-car parking structure.

The second phase includes a new 2400-seat performing arts worship auditorium and a 17,000-square-foot lobby and fellowship atrium. An extensive remodel of the existing facility includes children's youth spaces and administrative offices. The design features extensive rehearsal and studio spaces, large community rooms, and a gymnasium. The project also expanded the parking structure to accommodate 2500 spaces.

This project is part of a long-range masterplan, also designed by RNL, which includes a new ministry center and a special needs center to be constructed on their campus in the future.

The design strategy hinges upon phasing to make this project work. The owner wanted a performing arts type of space, yet had a limited budget. The owner felt that using the latest communications technology would improve outreach to the audience. The solution came in the masterplanning efforts. This initial phase provided the church with an infrastructure that could be adapted and expanded to meet future technology needs, providing the church with the opportunity to stay current with evolving technologies.

Additional challenges facing the design team were height limits and the footprint of the building. This was solved by using an auditorium with a linear shape, which is an advantage acoustically. Elevated seating areas and communications technology enhance intimacy in this space.

1

1 *Plan of the complex*
2 *Double-level entry*
3 *Sweeping reception lobby*
4 *Performing arts worship space*

Photography: Prakash Patel

2

3

4

East End Temple

BKSK Architects

A former New York City residence built in 1883 by renowned architect Richard Morris Hunt offered the East End Temple congregation and its architect an opportunity to create a richly layered, architecturally progressive space that expresses a vision of spirituality emerging out of the past with a modern sensibility.

The sanctuary embodies symbols of the Jewish faith, as well as the modern temple's inclusiveness. The volume of the space is lofty and cubic, as described in the book of Exodus for the first temple. The seating, oriented to true east, conforms to the strictest tenets of sanctuary design and also provides a quiet dynamic. Natural light, a symbol of divine presence, is brought in high over the ark with a ceiling designed as if its slabs were pulled apart to open a large fissure. Ten unique lights, representing the *minyan* required for a Jewish service, hang from the center of the Sanctuary at different heights.

The eternal light, the symbol of divine presence, has a frame that reads in alternating lines of Hebrew and English: "For God shall be a light to you forever." The metalwork of the eternal light is consistent with the gates, railings, and other metal objects designed for the project, which are found from the start of one's journey into the temple from the street, through the vestibule, and culminating in the eternal light in the sanctuary.

The cast bronze ark doors incorporate both traditional symbolism and congregant participation. The weave of the fabric used for casting recalls the Star of David and is entwined throughout with a vine of 12 leaves representing the original 12 tribes of Israel. Strips of paper with the congregation's prayers were thrown into the molten metal during the casting. On the door handles is written the literal and metaphorical statement: "Within these doors are cast the prayers and wishes of congregation El Emet."

1

1 Decorative metalwork starts at the entry
2 Sanctuary level plan
3 Seating around the corner bema
4 Ark's cast bronze doors
5 Eternal light inscription, in English and Hebrew
6 Sanctuary's delicate minyan lights

Photography: Jonathan Wallan

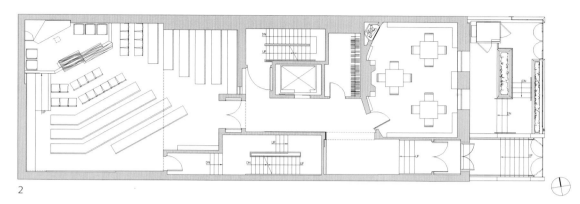

2

3

4

5

6

Riggo-Lynch Chapel

Maya Lin Studio
Bialosky + Partners, Associated Architect

The concept for the design of this chapel for the Children's Defense Fund at Haley Farm in Clinton, Tennessee, comes from the Fund's motto: "Dear Lord, be good to me. The sea is so wide, and my boat is so small."

The abstracted image of a boat or ark constructed of wood, which forms the main body of the chapel, is at the heart of the design. It is a reminder not only of the motto; it also gives a quiet yet unique center to all of Haley Farm—architecturally and spiritually.

The simple shape fits with the vernacular architecture of Haley Farm, yet it offers something special: a familiar form, yet different. The imagery of the boat is abstracted so that the design at times is seen as a clean architectural composition of both straight and gently curving lines, but at certain key points the boat-like shape is revealed, welcoming one to the Farm.

An open courtyard connects the entire design, linking the main body of the chapel to the administration rooms, grounding the design and creating a large gathering area for use even in inclement weather, when the sides can be closed to protect the area from sun or rain.

The need for flexible seating options led to centering the chapel around the large outdoor courtyard. The design is intimate yet allows the ability to seat more than twice the number of people at certain times of the year. The indoor/outdoor space allows the use of a tent to accommodate overflow seating.

The administrative wing, physically connected to the chapel yet visually separate from it, allows for all offices, service facilities, and additional meeting spaces to be highly flexible, suiting the multiple needs of Haley Farm.

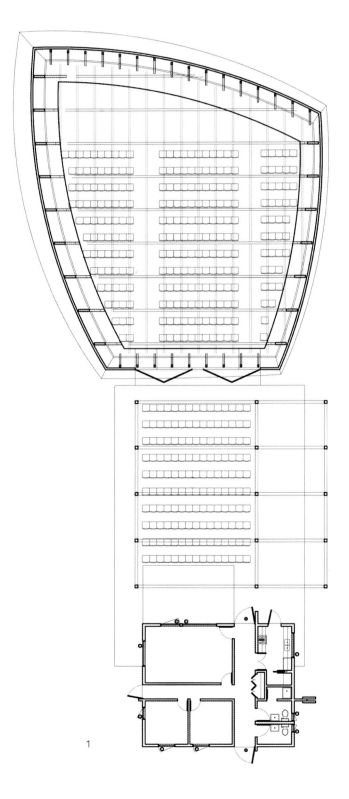

1   *Chapel level plan*

Opposite

Detail of the chapel's boat-like interior

1

3

4

5

6

Photography: Timothy Hursley; Maya Lim Studio

7

San Fernando Cathedral and Cathedral Centre

Rafferty Rafferty Tollefson Architects

On March 9, 1731, Spanish immigrants gathered in San Antonio, Texas, and established San Fernando Church in honor of the King of Spain's patron saint. From that first day, San Fernando Cathedral has stood at the center and soul of the City of San Antonio. The walls of the church, begun in 1738, still stand today to form the oldest Roman Catholic sanctuary in the U.S., with the oldest continuously active parish in Texas. In 1868, a French Gothic nave was callously added to the original Spanish Colonial structure creating the basic church as it stands today.

Rising damp moisture problems wicked from the ground into the stone structure had brought the 1738 Spanish Colonial structure to the verge of collapse. The poorly functioning facilities had brought the cathedral parish to the point of chaos. The entire structure and its supporting spaces underwent a complete restoration and upgrade with the assistance of liturgical design consultant Richard Vosko and Fisher Heck as associate architects.

The project underwent a complete replacement of all mechanical, electrical, lighting, plumbing, and sound systems. The entire structure was preserved through restoration and replacement as necessary of the masonry walls, the ceiling, roofs, and the interior/exterior stone and plaster.

The liturgical arrangement of the altar, the pulpit, the baptismal font, the choir, the bishop's cathedra, the seating, and the tabernacle were changed completely to accommodate a stronger sense of community liturgy. Artwork was restored, new artwork was commissioned, and some artwork was removed to give greater emphasis to the new and remaining pieces. Original ceilings were recreated and stained-glass windows were restored.

The new Cathedral Centre was built to create a community space for visitors, members of the parish, festivals, quiet contemplation, and support facilities to relieve the pressure of constant use on the cathedral itself.

1

2

1 *Side aisle displays restoration of décor*
2 *Cathedral Centre is found to the right of the cathedral*
3 *Building's old stone was cleaned and restored*

3

4

5

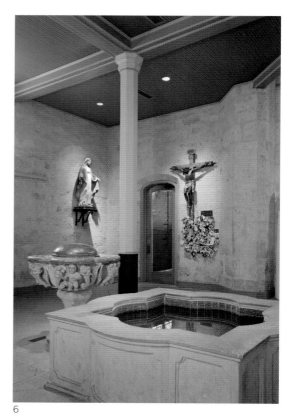

6

7

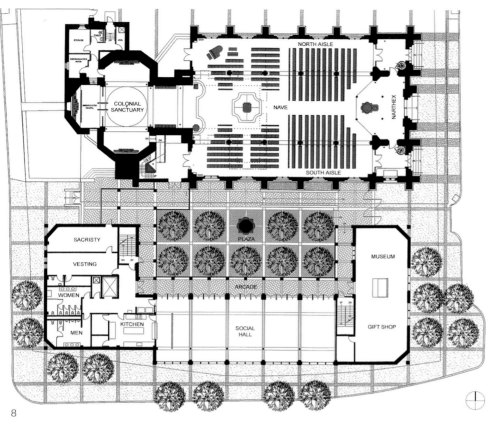

4 *Chapel to Our Lady of Guadalupe*
5 *Axial view of nave from entry*
6 *New baptismal font joins original font*
7 *New altar located nearer to congregation*
8 *Plan of church (above) and Cathedral Centre*
9 *Lighting accentuates wood ceiling structure*

Photography: Chris Cooper Photography

8

9

St. Croix Lutheran High School Chapel

Kodet Architectural Group

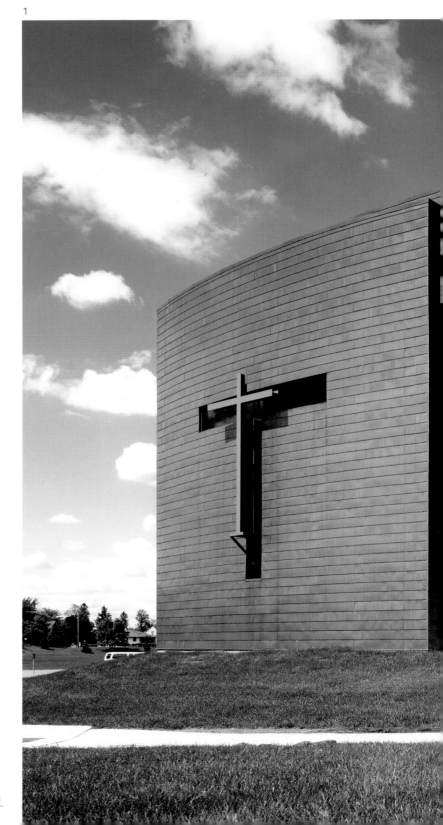

1

S t. Croix Lutheran High School in west St. Paul, Minnesota, believes in "educating the total student—spiritually, intellectually, physically—in a caring Christian family community." This new 500-seat chapel is an important element in the school's educational mission.

The chapel's form is a reflection of religious belief. The three semi-curved walls represent the Trinity. The simple metal brackets at the front of the building form an abstract interpretation of a human body supporting a cross.

The connection of light and space is evident throughout the chapel. The central altar platform is located on the main axis under a small light scoop to highlight the events taking place. Worshipers sit on all sides, close to the platform, facing each other to enhance the sense of community and interaction with the liturgy. The seating is flexible, reflecting the young, dynamic people whom the chapel serves. Also drawing the congregation's eyes toward the altar and the heavens is the exposed steel frame, capturing attention while supporting the structure. The progression of light and materials culminates in a slot window that emphasizes the exterior cross. Viewed from the interior, the building glows with radiant light.

Worship includes celebration through song and the spoken word, so acoustics are an important factor. To help control sound, each window at the side walls is angled as are the coffers above the space frame.

Copper is used because in certain ways it mirrors life's journey. When first installed, it is bright and contains all the promise of new life. Soon after exposure to the elements copper begins to mature. It takes on a more complex character and begins the aging process. Over the next 20 years it changes to brown and develops a patina and maturity. With more time it will change from brown to green and then completely to green, weathered from its productive life.

2

1 Copper is used extensively inside and out
2 Chapel interior glows with copper sheath

3 *Plan of chapel wing attached to high school building*
4 *Layered space is expressed on exterior*
5 *Altar is surrounded by seating on all sides*
Following pages
    Light, space, and warmth of copper material

Photography: Peter Bastianelli-Kerze; Edward J. Kordet, Jr, FAIA

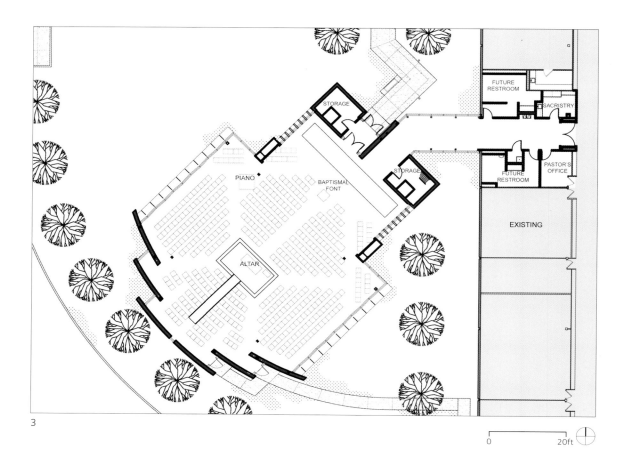

3

4

Tzemach Dovid Synagogue

Arcari & Iovino Architects

This small neighborhood synagogue for a congregation of 100 persons is located on the edge of a residential neighborhood in Teaneck, New Jersey. The residential structures in this community originate from the 1920s and 1930s, and are a mix of Craftsman and Tudor styles. Typical lot sizes are 50 by 100 feet, as is this site.

While the site alone would dictate that the resolution fit the scale of the neighborhood, the design challenge was to create a structure that reflected the character of the surrounding houses to appease the local zoning board, yet compose a building that was clearly not a house.

The client's program called for three primary spaces: worship, study, and gathering. Within the worship area there was to be ample yet controlled natural light with a visual separation from the busy street outside.

The solution evolved as a structure with three floors. By creating a sub-grade level for the study, which also serves as a play area for the youngest visitors, a zoning limitation of two stories above grade was met. The gathering space is entered at grade via front and rear entrances. The main and sub-grade levels allow the worship space to occupy the entire upper floor.

The building volume is clad in three basic materials: brick, metal, and stucco. The composition of these three, together with the thoughtful use of solids and voids, results in a form that reflects the programmatic elements inside. Converging shed roof lines at the stair towers and worship space emulate the "sloped-roof" character of the neighborhood while clearly being unique to this location.

The interiors are intentionally sparse in aesthetic quality. The clean lines of the walls and directed views outward and upward toward the mature trees create a interesting backdrop for the services.

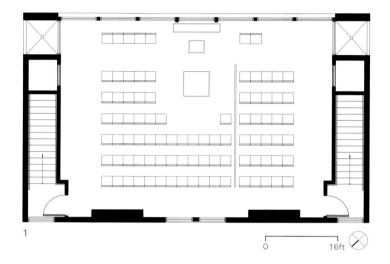

1

0   16ft

2

1   *Sanctuary level plan*

2   *Interior allows views up to mature trees*

Opposite

   Synagogue's compact form on small lot

Photography: James Shive

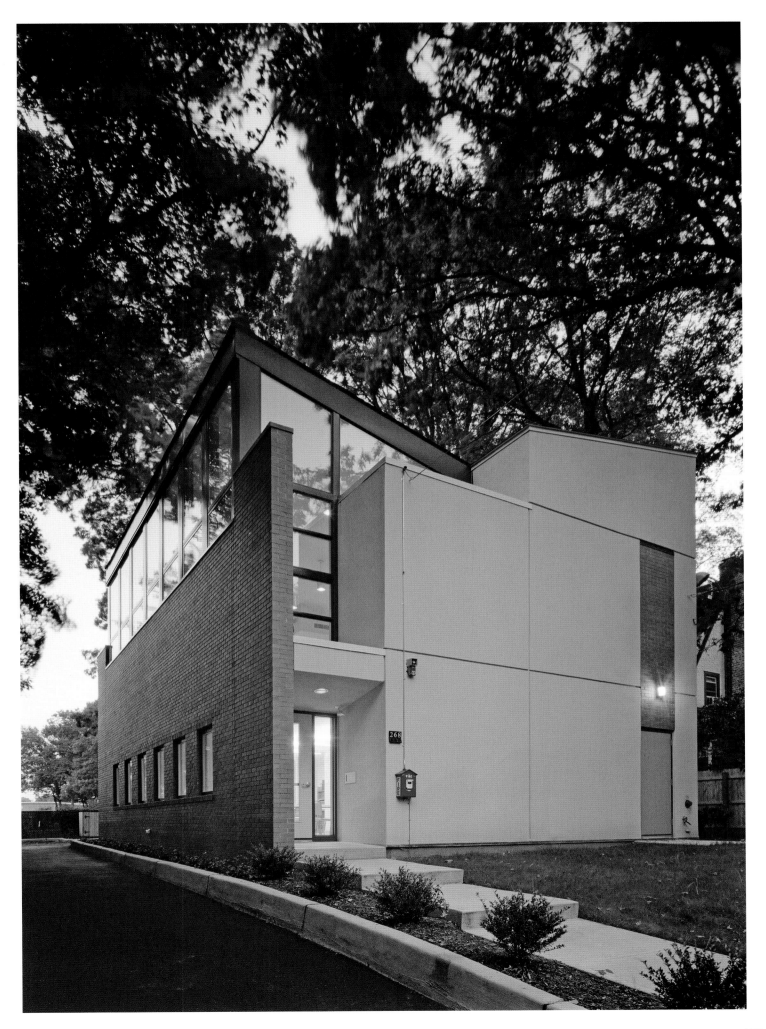

Center of Gravity Foundation Hall

Predock Frane Architects

The Center of Gravity Foundation Hall for the Bodhi Mandala Zen Center in Jemez Springs, New Mexico, serves as the primary teaching and meditation hall for the Zen Buddhist Compound. It is located in a high mountain river valley in Northern New Mexico with abundant geothermal activity below the site. The cliffs of the valley are rosy pink sculpted sandstone.

Conceptually, the project embraces oppositions; intersecting two embracing boxes—one of heaviness (rammed earth) and the other of lightness (polycarbonate on timber-strand) to define the transition from exterior to interior, and form the interior volume of the hall. The light, translucent west side "glows" with light as the sun sets over the mountains. The east side cradles the space with thick earthen walls, partially containing the "light" box. A folded, stealth-like metal roof plane hovers over the space supported by glulam beams and purlins. Primarily supported along the north and south ends, the east and west edges of the roof plane float above the walls, with clear glass filling this void. The cantilevers of this roof plane define raised exterior paths for walking meditation, and divert rainwater into a catchment for irrigation. Sliding panels along the east side open to reveal a 36-foot-wide aperture with foreground views onto a garden and background views toward the reddish mountains beyond.

The ritual and formality of traditional Zen practice is respected while the architecture establishes a new direction for the meeting of two foreign cultures. Monks and students "slip" between the earth walls and the layered polycarbonate walls as they enter the hall from opposite sides. The *Roshi* (teacher) enters from the east and sits in a *Teisho* chair facing the Buddha located within the blackened *budsudon* to the west. Monks sit on the north side facing the students in training to the south. Beyond the intense teaching seminars, ceremonies such as weddings and funerals also take place in the hall.

The heating and cooling is both passive and active. Passively, the thick compressed earth walls act as thermal composites, keeping unwanted summer heat out during the day and re-radiating it at night.

1

1   *Light slivers race across hall floor*

2   *Dynamic roof form appears in flight*

3   *Muscular structure supports broad roof*

2

3

4

5

6

4 *Interior has screen-like divisions*
5 *Glulam structure with purlins above*
6 *Hall presents a contemplative, restful space*
7 *Polycarbonate walls contrast with rammed earth*

Photography: Jason Predock

7

Perpetual Adoration Chapel
Holy Trinity Church

Bass Architects

Perpetual Adoration Chapel in West Harwich, Massachusetts, is a small but stunning building that is in constant, continual use for prayer and meditation. It is designed around a magnificent set of nine 100-year-old stained-glass windows made by F.X. Zettler of Bavaria. The architect drew inspiration from ancient country churches, particularly St. Etienne in Vignory, France, and designed a chapel that would appear to be a thousand years old but would meet all of the modern needs of its users.

The main church is a casual, shingled "seashore" style building befitting its Cape Cod location and its busy parish of approximately 1800 families and thousands of summer visitors. The 900-square-foot chapel sits on a secluded, wooded two-acre site behind the main sanctuary, separate from the main church in shape, design, purpose, and mood.

The chapel is dedicated solely to 24-hour prayer in an unbroken chain of one-hour shifts. The interior frames the priceless windows, salvaged from St. Matthew's Church in Fall River and donated by the bishop. Other requirements were that the chapel provide a comfortable place for worshippers, many of whom are elderly or disabled.

The chapel is built of New Hampshire granite trimmed with Indiana limestone, with an exposed roof structure of heavy timber trusses. Although the stained-glass windows established the major design elements of the building, the interior space highlights the altar and offers worshippers a spiritually directed setting. The intimacy of the space encourages one to lift the eyes upward. Pointed arches, a repeated quatrefoil pattern, a raised marble sanctuary, a painting of the heavens on the ceiling around the apse, and the various angel statues all help establish a sweeping, uplifting feeling.

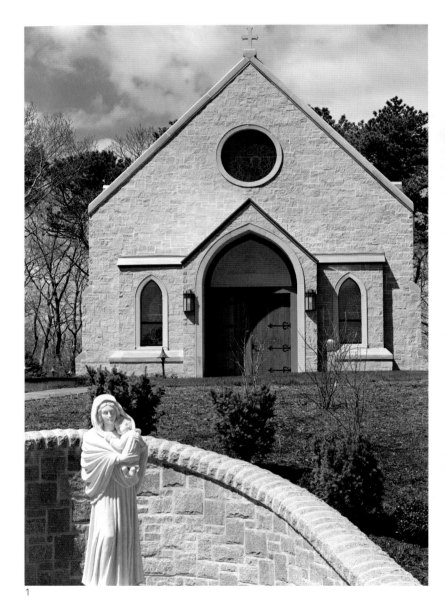
1

1 Chapel accentuates traditional liturgical design
2 Three of the antique windows used in new building
3 Interior focus is on Eucharistic adoration
4 Traditional details of altar railing
5 Classically composed sculptures of angels
6 Pointed arches are found throughout chapel

Photography: Kenneth M. Wyner

4

2

5

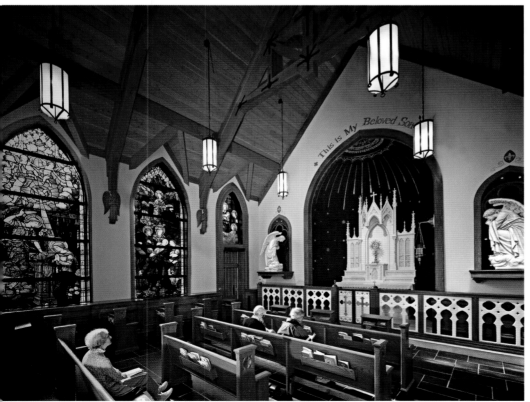
3

6

Congregation of Har Shalom Synagogue

WMCRP Architects

This first phase of an overall masterplan to expand this existing synagogue in Potomac, Maryland, includes a new 700-seat sanctuary, gathering hall, and small chapel. The masterplan calls for a sacred axis, with the library at one end and the sanctuary at the other, connected with a main hallway. The forms reinforce this axis and suggest the indigenous architecture of the Middle East in a modern language. The graphic concept for the building plan is a circle and a line.

The design solution begins with fixed benches arranged in concentric circles focused on the central bema. A linear axis interrupts the circles or rings of seats from the entry doors to the raised bema at the east end containing the *Aron Kodesh* (ark). This sacred axis is given architectural expression by a parallel wall clad in Jerusalem stone running from the entry gathering hall, through the sanctuary, to a garden to the east. The wall, a reference to the walled city of Jerusalem, organizes the forms used to enclose the worship space. On the south side, a partial dome rests against the wall. On the north side, a series of stepped roof clerestory forms provide views to the trees and sky that is so important to the congregation.

Wood glulam arched beams form the principal structure that supports the clerestories. These members introduce the wood ceiling, a modern interpretation of the old wooden synagogues of Eastern Europe. These "lost wooden synagogues" were designed in a vernacular style and had elaborately stepped roofs. Inside, an independent wood lattice ceiling with arches and vaulted forms symbolically recalls the tent-like structures of ancient times.

The ark, rendered in glass, wood, and brass, offers several readings of the Torah. It is designed to enhance the ritual of the Jewish Torah service, which involves a careful revealing of the sacred scrolls through the opening and closing of the ark doors.

1

2

3

1 *Dome form rests against the wall of the synagogue*

2 *Stepped form allows maximum light and views*

3 *Wall extends across the building and through it*

4 *Glass, wood, and metal ark against glass wall*

4

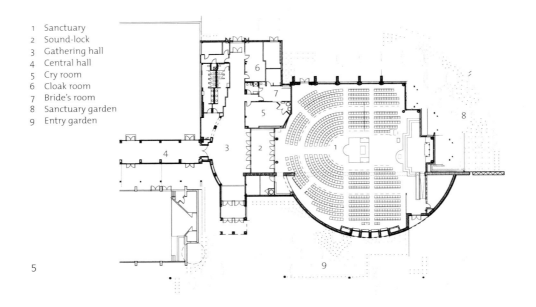

1 Sanctuary
2 Sound-lock
3 Gathering hall
4 Central hall
5 Cry room
6 Cloak room
7 Bride's room
8 Sanctuary garden
9 Entry garden

5

6

7

Photography: Kenneth M. Wyner

8

Church of St. François de Molitor

Jean-Marie Duthilleul – AREP, Architects

The Church of St. François stands on Rue Molitor in the 16th arrondissement of Paris, hovering between city and garden— two of the chief loci of the biblical sphere. City and garden are also two of the key realms of the life of St. Francis of Assisi, to whom the church is dedicated.

Running alongside the street stands the presbytery, a large, simple volume of translucent white marble, a color that blends well with the surrounding houses, the precious nature of the material reflecting the sacred character of the location. At night the translucent marble transforms the volume into an immense beacon.

Three monumental wooden doors lead to the narthex. Upon entering one sees the garden through a milky glass wall as through a mist. In front of the glass wall, a large cross stands facing the entrance, lit from the south through the glass roof. Standing in front of the cross on this north-south axis is the ambo and the pulpit. A large baptismal font is positioned to welcome the newly baptized into the community.

It is on the line drawn between the city and the garden that the Communion table, around which the congregation gathers, has been placed. To highlight this spot, the ground has been hollowed out, reminiscent of a ship's hold, or of two hands cupped to collect water from a spring. Around this area two curved masonry walls built from the honey-colored ashlar used everywhere in Paris embrace the congregation.

Two side galleries extend the enveloping sweep of the walls around the altar upwards, providing seating for 420 worshippers. The rays of light passing through the flat ceiling of loose planking illuminate the congregation and the altar, creating a sense of mystery and serenity.

To the east, three doors lead into a tiny tabernacle chapel, an inner sanctum symbolizing the beginning and end of the earthly life of Christ, where the faithful may come to pray and encounter the divine at all times of the day.

1

1   *Marble and wood distinguish exterior*

Opposite

Translucent glass wall lends ethereal quality

3

4

5

3   *Congregants pass by font to enter sanctuary*
4   *Seating bends around altar-like cupped hands*
5   *Natural materials are simple throughout*
6   *Upper-level seating and contemplative spaces*

Photography: Didier Boy de la Tour

6

Thrivent Chapel

LEO A DALY

This chapel fronts on the main lobby of Thrivent Financial's prominent downtown Minneapolis, Minnesota, Corporate Center. The chapel provides employees and the public with a retreat from the hectic work-a-day world and is symbolic of Thrivent's religious and spiritually based business activities, greeting employees and visitors as they enter the facility. The client requested a design of elegant simplicity.

The chapel's form and materials stand apart from and respect the existing public area's monolithic materials and clean, masculine lines of the 1970's modernist office building. The soft, rounded forms of the chapel project into the rectilinear lobby with curving feminine lines, warm and inviting.

The chapel has curved Venetian plaster walls, coupled with natural slate, hickory benches and woodwork, and sisal flooring to provide an envelope of comfort, seclusion, and reflection. Soft, translucent, wave-patterned art-glass shields the room's occupants from public view, while suggesting to the passerby that this is a unique space worthy of investigation.

The chapel design revolves around the vigil light as a welcoming and centering device, physically and spiritually. The light of textured red slump glass is invitingly visible to the main entry lobby through a narrow slit left as the curving chapel wall rolls up and away from the lobby.

The chapel vestibule is a transitional area where one leaves the busy, public work-world and enters the chapel. The space compresses and envelops the visitor with warm hickory wood and intimate contact with the vigil light. The chapel opens up in welcome, the curved walls holding the user as between two hands.

The solitary, rustically formed bronze cross and the Paul Granlund sculpture, "Dancing at the Presence of God", share the space with the users. Mark Anderson and Justin Wilwerding served as liturgical design consultants on the project.

1   Chapel layout
2   Door to chapel wing invites passersby
3   Chapel's curved form reaches out
4   Interior space is oval and contemplative
5   Sculpture is a presence in the chapel

Photography: George Heinrich

1

1	Chapel	4	Employee entry
2	Vestibule	5	Lobby
3	Vigil Light	6	Elevator corridor

2

3

4

5

St. Francis de Sales Catholic Church

Rafferty Rafferty Tollefson Architects

The site for this new church is a century-old dairy farm in Morgantown, West Virginia, on a flat knoll with a panoramic view of the surrounding hills and valleys. The site is a rolling pasture with some rock outcroppings, steeply sloping down 75 feet at the middle to the east. This slope's natural edge forms the panoramic view. The barn, set on this prominent point, is a local landmark for all who pass on the highway below.

The new church complex explores the concept of community through the individual expression of the many parish functions. St. Francis de Sales is more an expression of church as a community rather than church as building. The sanctuary, the largest element, is set back to allow the other elements of administration, meeting spaces, social hall, daily chapel, and kitchen to be expressed. These five new structures form a cluster built around the original barn. Their architectural forms explore variations on the barn's vernacular architectural image. Each element is as important architecturally for the whole as they are functionally for the parish.

Viewed from a distance or up close, there is significant variety in the massing and placement of the forms, but all of the elements borrow from the rural vernacular character of the original barn, which has been preserved, modified, and serves as the new social hall. The barn's roof and its delicate wood structure, near the failing point, were reinforced with steel and the middle portion of the hayloft floor was removed to create an open mezzanine. The irregularly shaped flat-roofed gathering space is divided into two levels to enhance the viewing opportunities of the panoramic view. All entries to the complex bring the community together at this point in the same manner that a piazza or central plaza would for a village.

1

1   *Existing barn before new construction*
2   *New complex is a community of agrarian forms*
3   *Entry leads to central plaza of community*
4   *Rural architecture inspired new buildings*

2

3

4

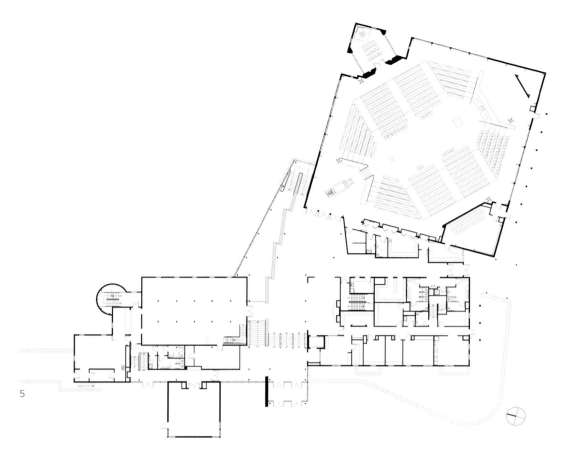

5

6

5 Worship level plan
6 New worship space with large font
7 Church recalls barn-like roof structure
8 Existing barn is now a parish hall
9 Daily chapel adjacent to worship space

Photography: Steve Bergerson

7

8

9

St. Mary of the Springs Chapel

Nagle Hartray Danker Kagan McKay Penney

St. Mary of the Springs is the new home for a congregation of Dominican Sisters with national and international ministries. The heavily wooded site in Columbus, Ohio, features rolling topography. The program includes 90 resident rooms, central dining, a chapel, congregation offices, and ministry outreach facilities.

The sisters undertook this project to foster a sense of community for their aging congregation and to facilitate outreach ministries. Resident rooms are clustered around community living and dining rooms. Clusters of rooms are organized around a landscaped courtyard that minimizes interior travel distances and provides a secure outdoor environment.

The chapel is the focus of daily community life. The new chapel replaces a below-grade chapel that has since been remodeled into a conference room to further the congregation's outreach ministries. The new chapel reflects the aspirations and values of the community it serves.

The chapel's rectangular plan provides flexibility for worship, funeral, and other religious services. The design in section recalls historic cathedral designs. Traditional buttresses are inverted to support curving masonry walls that define the side aisles. The buttresses also give expression to the chapel on the exterior.

Curving walls and natural materials impart a sacred and organic character reflecting the spirit of this community, like a bud opening from the soil. Natural interior finishes include molded brick, cast stone, Douglas fir wood trusses and ceilings, and oak floors.

Ornamental flourishes further distinguish the chapel as a reflection of this religious community. Buttress caps are carved with an abstract water pattern. Herringbone flooring echoes the water theme. Stained-glass windows designed by a member of the congregation reflect biblical stories concerning water. Windows facing east and west cast colored light into the space during daily services. A circular stained glass window in the south wall illustrates the Dominican star and echoes traditional rose windows. Chapel forms and materials are introduced by a bell tower that greets visitors at the main entry.

1

1   Bell tower greets visitors near entry
2   Worship space abounds with natural materials
3   Section indicates curved masonry walls
4   Chapel exterior with organic, curved walls

2

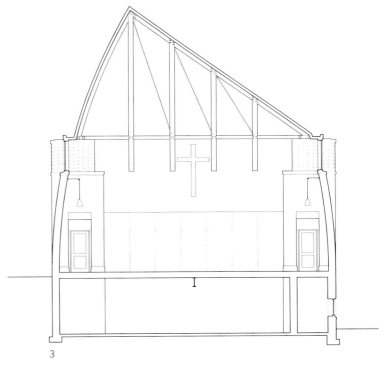

3

4

5 *Plan is organized around a courtyard*
6 *Movable seating allows flexibility*
7 *Lighting detail in wood truss*

Opposite

North wall has expansive window

Photography: Brad Feinknopf;
  Scott McDonald © Hedrich Blessing

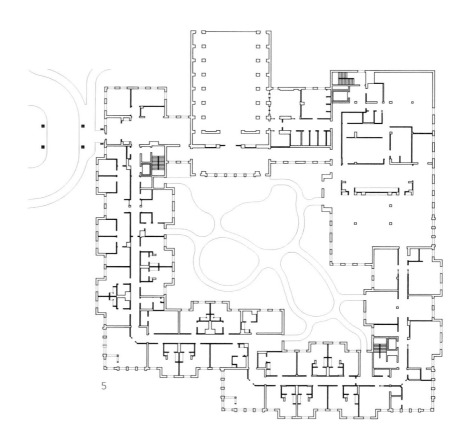

5

7

6

St. Paul the Apostle Church

Vincent Benic Architect

A combination of traditional church design with current Church theology and modern materials and methods distinguishes this Catholic church in Corona, Queens, New York. While keeping those elements in mind, the design of the church is derived from the congregation's set priorities and site influences, all the while keeping to a tight budget.

The existing site is surrounded by low to medium-density housing to the west and south. Across the street to the north is an industrial site. Just east of the parish hall, where the existing church is located, a new assisted living facility was to be built on land sold by the church. This limited the location of any new building on the existing parish hall site to the west of the hall.

Many different approaches for locating the new church were studied—everything from converting the existing auditorium, or adding on to it, to building a separate, free-standing building. While the last option was the most desirable, the cost made it the least viable. Both the architects and members of the congregation felt that adding on to the existing parish hall was the best compromise because existing elements such as heating and cooling mechanical equipment, plumbing, and the structural framework could be shared, while the church has the freedom to function independently from the hall. The design of the church also responded to other desires of the congregation, such as a large seating and gathering area, a building independent from the existing parish hall, and a church with a strong architectural presence in the community.

The sanctuary space can seat more than 350 people with the possibility for overflow, while the vestibule acts as a gathering space. The interior spaces combine modern materials and the spatial drama of Gothic cathedrals to create a space that celebrates the church and its community. The architects introduced a tower to the design, which allows the church to appear separate from the parish hall. A strong architectural presence for the church in the community is created by the tower.

1

1 Welcoming entry approached from east
2 Church elevation is spare but powerful
3 Section through sanctuary
4 Worship level plan
5 Seating arrayed around the altar is intimate
6 Glass block behind the altar reaches to the heavens

Photography: Seong Kwon

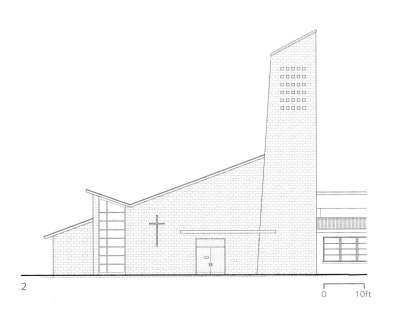

2

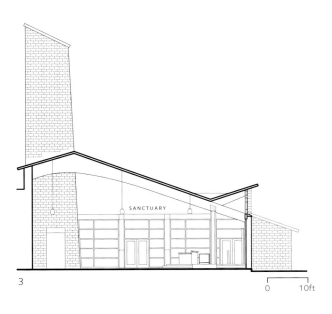

3

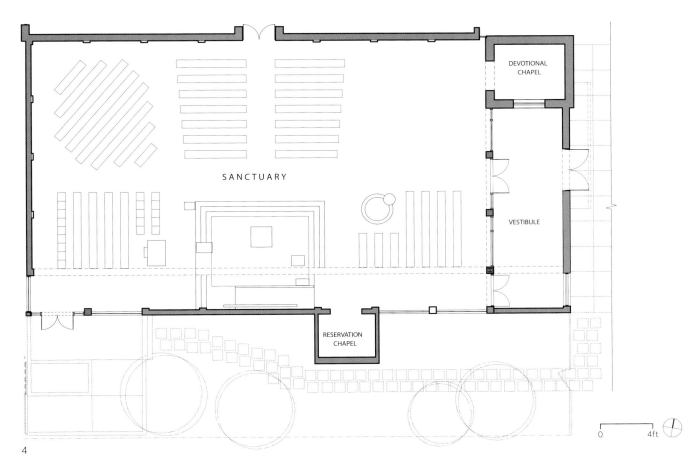

DEVOTIONAL
CHAPEL

VESTIBULE

SANCTUARY

RESERVATION
CHAPEL

4

5

6

Northminster Presbyterian Church Renovation

Olson Sundberg Kundig Allen Architects

The members of this small congregation in Seattle, Washington, sought to enhance the sense of participation in their worship experience by reinforcing the chancel of their 1960's church as the focal point (the altar table, the font, and the ambo in particular).

The existing church had a classic 1960's interior, with laminated arches, exposed masonry, and a sanctuary somewhat removed from the congregation. The design approach was to help soften the hard edges of the sanctuary's existing elements, and to create a more intimate sense of community between those in the sanctuary and the nave. A neutral white background on the back of the chancel wall allows the celebrant and other liturgical participants to come to the fore, making the distance between them and the congregants more compressed.

The new design removes extraneous elements that had crept into the chancel over time and introduces a simple, unifying background. The new, open chancel makes use of flexible platforms to accommodate a variety of activities including worship, communion, weddings, liturgical dance, and musical events, as well as access for the disabled. Light-colored woods used in the platforms and the liturgical furnishings further help to expand the space visually. The altar area was brought forward toward the congregation. Its oval platform is a soft form that helps to modulate the hard lines of the structure.

To help modulate the harsh natural light coming into the nave, fabric scrims were installed on the inside of the windows. The light-colored scrims soften the natural light and help to unify the sanctuary visually, directing attention to the chancel and the minister.

1   *Lectern incorporates clean, modern lines*
2   *Font is in keeping with buoyant interior*
3   *Altar was moved toward congregation*
4   *Window scrims modulate natural light*
5   *Balanced interior light reduces glare*

Photography: Tim Bies

3

4

5

Merle & Marjorie Fish Interfaith Center

AC Martin Partners

This chapel at Chapman University in Orange, California, offers spaces that transport visitors from the material world of the campus into the spiritual realm. The symbols used in this journey had to comfortably accommodate people of many different beliefs, which ruled out the use of traditional religious iconography. The symbols selected are those that bind religions together, such as light, water, and the universe. To achieve this interfaith vision, the architect collaborated with five prominent artists.

The journey begins with a 60-foot light tower that glows with lantern-like illumination from backlit marble. This beacon is a focal point, drawing the visitor onto a pathway that leads to the chapel. The entry door, created by another artist, has glass with bronze panels representing the wholeness of life.

Inside, light spills into the vestibule laterally, filling the lower part of the space with constantly varying light and shadow. Farther into the corridor the light enters from above as the glass windows on the wall, laminated with rice paper, become more opaque.

The main sanctuary is voluminous, bathed in filtered light. Above the altar is a golden-bronze metal sculpture portraying the setting moon and rising sun. Light from the skylight and colored glass windows interweaves with interior lighting to play upon the sculpture's surface. On the dais beneath the sculpture, custom designed furniture and carpet further the celestial metaphor with designs inspired by Hubble telescope images. The sanctuary has only one view to the outside through a small window. The view is of a small maple tree in the Garden of the Senses.

Varying sources and colors of light reflect through windows set in the thick curving walls. Colored light within the sanctuary constantly changes, complemented by a variety of subtly colored patterned light resulting from intricately designed floor-to-ceiling windows at each corner of the space. The windows' translucent panes are overlaid with etched iridescent glass. The chapel roof is separated from the walls by a continuous strip of glass, creating a band of soft, white light that makes the roof appear to float.

1

1 *Vestibule leading to chapel*
Opposite
   Chapel reaches out to visitors with trellis

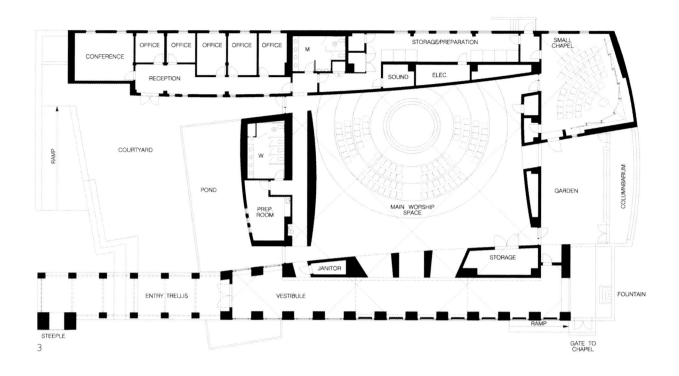

3

3 Worship level plan
4 Columbarium near chapel's garden
5 Chapel is filled with light and art
6 Inset windows diffuse color to interior
7 Detail of window in curved chapel wall

Photography: Tim Griffith

4

5

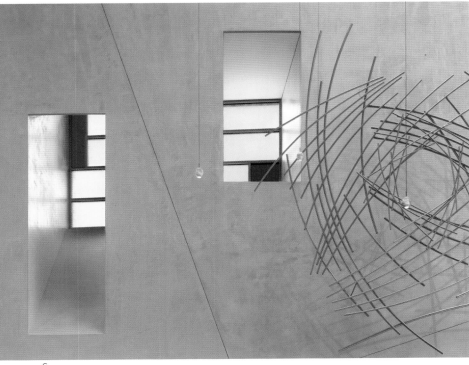

6

7

Sacred Heart Cathedral Restoration and Additions

Williamson Pounders Architects

The restoration of and additions to this 75-year-old inner-city Gothic Revival cathedral in Rochester, New York, bring it into full conformance with contemporary Roman Catholic liturgical standards and provide major new spaces for social gatherings, meetings, and administration. The work, completed with the assistance of Richard Vosko as liturgical consultant and the local architecture firm of LaBella Associates, includes complete restoration of the cathedral interior and design of important new liturgical focal points.

A granite baptismal font was added inside the worship space near the main entrance. A new granite altar now occupies the crossing of the nave and transepts, bringing it closer to the congregation. The painted plaster walls, sculptures, and elaborately decorated ceiling were restored to create a warmer, more unified scheme. Old pews were removed and replaced with chairs for greater flexibility and a new tile floor was installed. In the existing sanctuary area, the old altar was dismantled and the space reconfigured for an expanded choir and a future pipe organ. A new Blessed Sacrament chapel was created and features gold leaf constellations on its ceiling. New reconciliation chapels with a skylit entry vestibule were added, the original stained glass windows were restored, and the confessional booths were converted into shrines for a number of saints. An obsolete organ was removed and the balcony reconfigured to provide overflow seating. Air conditioning and a new sound-reinforcement system were added, and the old pendant light fixtures were replaced by a new computer-controlled lighting system.

The new narthex, inserted into a former courtyard between the nave and the neighboring rectory, unifies the cathedral complex. It allows centralized access to the cathedral, rectory, and a new office wing, and provides improved exterior entrances and a generous informal gathering space. Views of the upper façade of the cathedral are framed through the clerestory windows.

A new front entry plaza includes generous steps, lighting, and a ramp for full access. Other site improvements include two new neighborhood parks, a parking lot, and a porte cochere.

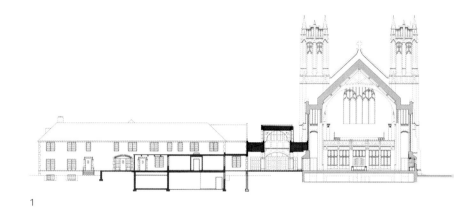

1

2

1   Section through new narthex
2   Accessible ramp leads to entry plaza
3   Centrally located altar table

3

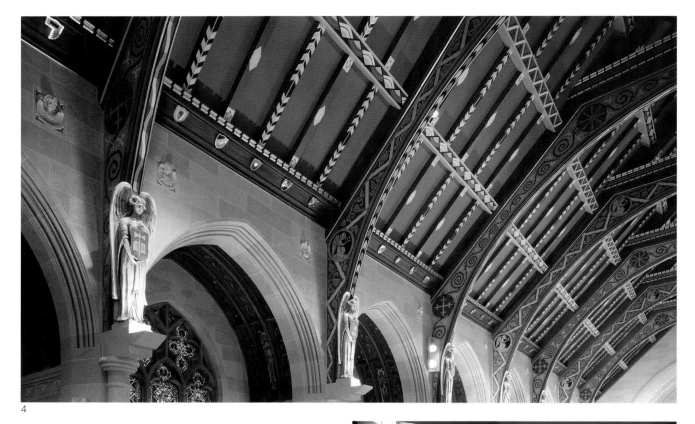

4

5

4 Decorative flourishes were carefully restored
5 Narthex joins cathedral with administration
6 New font is positioned near entry
7 Chapel decorated with stars in gold leaf
8 Sanctuary level plan
9 Movable seating allows flexibility

Photography: Tim Wilkes Photography; James F. Williamson, FAIA

6

7

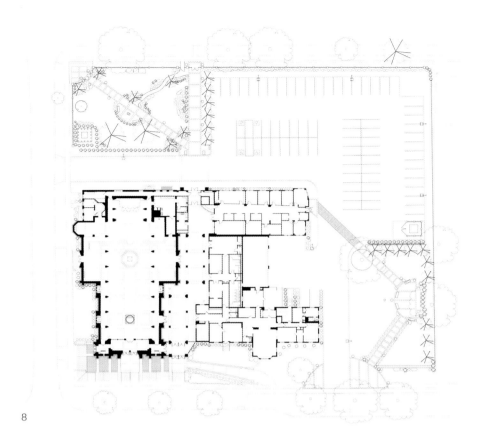

8

9

Grace Chapel at St. Mark's Episcopal Church

Jackson & McElhaney Architects

Grace Chapel in Austin, Texas, is designed as ancillary worship space to the main sanctuary of St. Mark's Episcopal Church. With seating for up to 80, it also functions as a choir rehearsal room and meeting space. Along with its diminutive worship space, the chapel also includes a classroom space that opens onto an outdoor deck, and two offices.

The chapel, which is used for children's Sunday services, is sited adjacent to a playground and is attached to the south end of an existing parish hall. The chapel and the main sanctuary, found on the other side of the parish hall, help to define a generous, south-facing courtyard.

The chapel space itself is intimate yet expansive. It is open and airy, yet private to the street. The chapel's sloping wall of glass under its soaring roof faces the street (southeast side) as a welcoming window to the community. Opposite the glass wall are rustic stone walls. At night, the glassy chapel casts an inviting, lantern-like glow seen by all who enter the only access street to this Austin neighborhood.

The chapel space is given a measure of privacy by a curved, wooden fence that is punctuated with a central stone columbarium wall. This feature recalls the traditional churchyard cemetery and meditation garden. The exposed wood ceilings, stone walls, clay tile floors, and glass provide a warm natural palette of materials that helps to meld the chapel with the wooded site and blend it with the existing stone sanctuary.

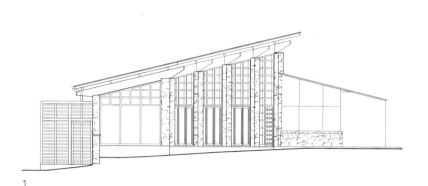

1

2

1 *Section through chapel*
2 *Roof gives chapel a soaring appearance*
3 *Columbarium/garden is found to left*

3

4 *Connection from church to chapel*
5 *Native stone recalls local architecture*
Opposite
  Ceiling provides uplifting space

Photography: Greg Hursley

4

5

Beth Sholom Synagogue

Finegold Alexander + Associates

The conservative congregation of the Beth Sholom Synagogue had outgrown its existing worship space and commissioned the design of this new synagogue to accommodate its 400 families. The congregation, in partnership with a local day school, purchased a 7.3-acre site in a residential neighborhood of Memphis, Tennessee. Each institution built its own facility independently, but the two share certain exterior public spaces.

The new 25,250-square-foot synagogue satisfies a number of objectives, including the creation of a structure that is compatible with the design of the neighboring school. The exterior of buff-colored brick, white trim, and dark windows is institutional in bearing, but it does not appear overtly religious. The two-story-high wing with the broad, overhanging roof houses the sanctuary.

One enters the synagogue from the south, past a small administration component, into a large lobby area or "community court," with the social hall to the west and the sanctuary to the east. The sanctuary seats 620, with expansion room to accommodate 750 on high holy days. This cube-like space is buoyant, with a roof that seems to float above a band of windows. There is balcony seating on the north and south sides of the sanctuary.

A chapel, designed for smaller gatherings of no more than 50, is located just north of the sanctuary, off the community court. This circular space with light woodwork features eight stained-glass windows taken from the older synagogue. The chapel's bema is the focus of this space, with the ark located on the east wall.

1

1   Circular chapel displays antique windows
2   Synagogue exterior is not overly religious
3   Sanctuary level plan

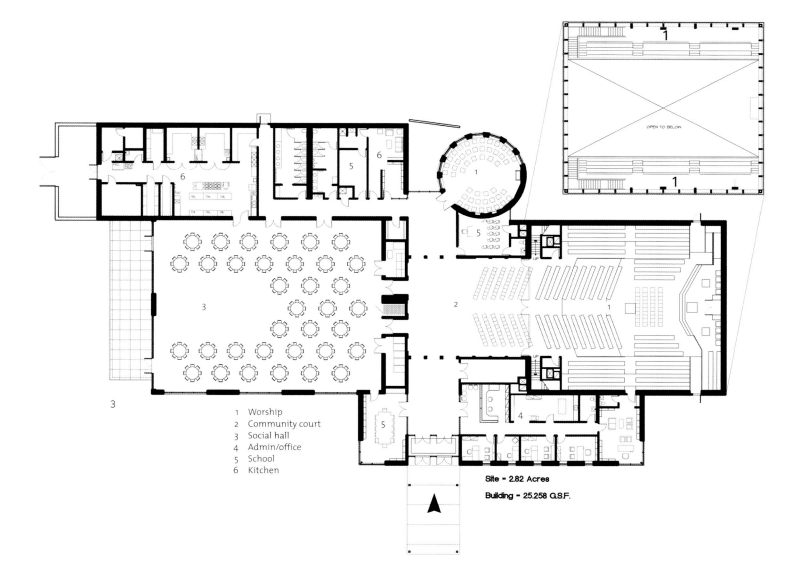

1 Worship
2 Community court
3 Social hall
4 Admin/office
5 School
6 Kitchen

Site = 2.82 Acres

Building = 25.258 G.S.F.

4 *"Community court" with sanctuary beyond*

5 *Sanctuary with its "floating" roof*

Opposite

   Ark is incorporated into east wall

Photography: Jeffrey Jacobs

4

5

עבדו את־יהוה בשמחה באו לפניו ברננה

St. John the Baptist Catholic Church

Edwards & Daniels Architects

St. John the Baptist Catholic Church is the last major development at the Skagg's Catholic Center, a 56-acre campus that also accommodates Juan Diego Catholic High School and St. John the Baptist Middle and Elementary Schools. Framing the main entrance to the campus, this church contains an 850-seat worship space (the second largest Catholic worship space in Utah), offices, and meeting areas.

The functional program of the church includes the principal worship space, a reservation chapel, a reconciliation room, a baptistery, a children's chapel, and a small meditation chapel. A large gathering space/narthex serves as pre- and post-function meeting area as well as an overflow space for the nave area. The administrative area supports the pastoral staff and includes offices, meeting rooms, a library, and workrooms.

St. John the Baptist is a careful synthesis of traditional Roman Catholic architecture and the modern aesthetic of the existing Skagg's Catholic Center. It employs the strong axial disposition, structural rigor, and use of light found in historic church basilicas, re-interpreted using contemporary architectural vocabulary.

The building form establishes a strong axial disposition that leads one through progressively more sacred spaces. At one end of the axis is the gathering space, viewable by the passing public as an invitation to the communal celebrations of the parish. At the opposite end of this axis reside the principal liturgical elements—the altar, ambo, font, and tabernacle. This area is more closed and protected to create a sense of sanctuary around the liturgical centers. The connecting space, housing the nave and side aisles, has a strong processional arrangement, augmented by the linearity, rhythm, angled walls, and forced perspective of the architecture.

Height limits imposed by local building ordinances precluded conventional pitched roof forms. To create an appropriate roof form for the worship area, the architects chose an arched roof that recalls both the vaulting of medieval church buildings and the graceful tents of the earliest Judeo-Christian worship spaces. The vaulted ceiling also exploits natural light, provides excellent natural acoustics, and creates a sacred experience.

1

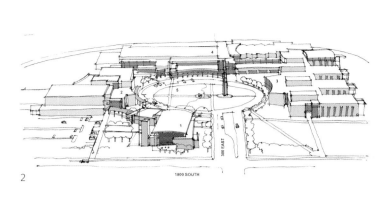

2

3

1   Luminous church with its landmark tower
2   Overview of church complex
3   Church as it faces entry to complex

4 Curved ceiling recalls tent structures

5 Worship level plan

6 Large narthex leads to sanctuary

7 Stained glass window near altar

8 Welcoming and comfortable gathering space

9 Side aisles animated with stained glass

10 Altar area is raised for better view

Photography: Jon Denker

4

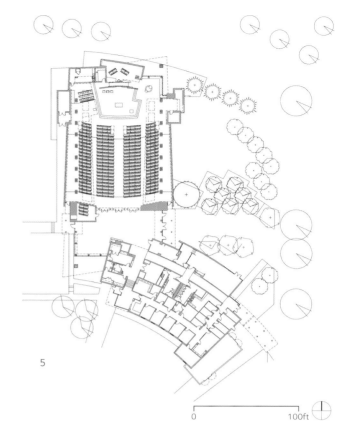

5

0   100ft

6

7

8

9

10

Bigelow Chapel, United Theological Seminary

Hammel, Green and Abrahamson

B igelow Chapel at the United Theological Seminary in New Brighton, Minnesota, realizes the client's request for a timeless, spiritually uplifting, ecumenical worship space.

The 5300-square-foot building, which includes a processional, narthex, chapel, and bell tower, serves a multi-denominational community of students, faculty, staff, and visitors. The chapel is wrapped in curvilinear, quilted maple: the floors, the ceiling panels that overlap to create a canopy over the processional and the sanctuary, and the six vertical panels that flow like ribbons along the interior of the west glass-and-stainless steel curtain wall all combine to create a cocoon-like sense of intimacy.

Thin maple veneers are sandwiched between sheets of clear, non-reflective acrylic in order to filter and modulate light coming through the glass wall. To achieve this effect, one big-leaf maple tree from the Pacific Northwest was shipped to Germany to be peeled, then shipped back to Indiana and cut into thin veneer strips, which were then laminated between two sheets of acrylic.

A quality of weightlessness—or lightness—is achieved through the use of slender, floating forms. The thin suspended planes of the glass fins and curving maple panels are echoed in the narthex roof (which cantilevers nearly 20 feet into space) and the elegant, freestanding 40-foot-high twin walls of the bell tower. A narrow cross emanates from the bell tower's cream-colored wall, while a similar cross is incised in the south wall of the sanctuary. A window on the south wall overlooks a meditation garden created by landscape architect Shane Coen, Coen + Partners of Minneapolis.

The building's cast-stone walls incorporate an inventive use of precast concrete. Originally, the design called for a split-face Italian travertine. Instead, 50 pieces of travertine were used to create rubber molds to cast the 4000 replica precast concrete "stones" that cover the exterior.

1

1   *View toward sanctuary space within*
2   *Building's precast concrete appears as stone*
3   *Cantilevered narthex roof*
4   *Sanctuary is between tower and narthex*

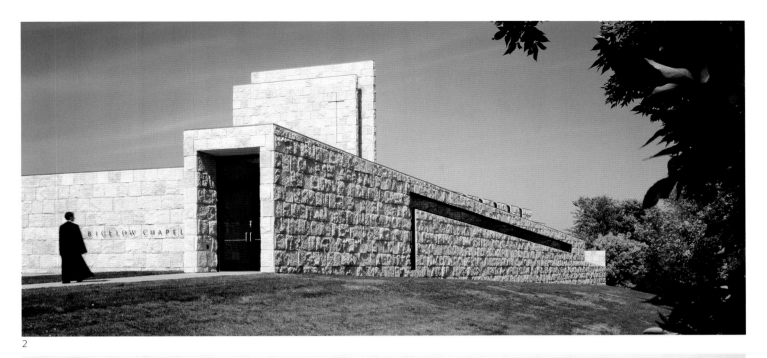

2

3

4

5 *Curved acrylic and wood panels create "cocoon"*
6 *Promenade is filled with natural light*

Photography: Paul Warchol

5

House of Prayer Lutheran Church

Bechtel Frank Erickson Architects

Set in historic Hingham, Massachusetts, this project consists of an addition and renovation to a 1960's church structure. The congregation expressed a need for expanding the sanctuary and narthex spaces, augmenting the social hall, and providing classrooms and a nursery for Sunday school. The design team located the nave, narthex, and sacristy in a new structure, while renovating the existing building to house a fellowship hall, the church offices, and classrooms. The new massing provides an opportunity to create a church with a stronger "visual presence" than existed with the original structure.

The two separate structures are unified by a tower marking the entry from the parking area and the glass curtain wall marking the passageway between the two parts. The original construction was clad with painted "Texture 1-11" plywood. The two structures are now clad with a stucco finish for ease of maintenance. The material imbues the buildings with a more monumental, less historicized, appearance.

The interiors are simple and spacious. The new sanctuary has a side entrance to provide an intimate relationship between the parishioners and the altar. The quality of light in the space was considered for the relocation of the stained glass windows as well as the comfort of the parishioners. A highlight of the new sanctuary is the naturally illuminated cross behind the altar. The floors are black polished concrete and carpet. The ceiling and walls are painted gypsum wallboard with a textured paint used on the ceiling.

A central mission for the Church was to create an environment to serve the congregation and the community through social ministry programs: spreading the Christian message and its promise of fellowship and good news. With the new fellowship hall, classrooms, and expanded nave and narthex, membership has increased by 30 percent. With this growth, the church not only fulfills its mission, but also helps sustain and enhance the vitality of the congregation.

1

2

1 *Section through sanctuary and tower*
2 *New church is a collection of forms*
Opposite
   Interior of soothing color and light

5

6

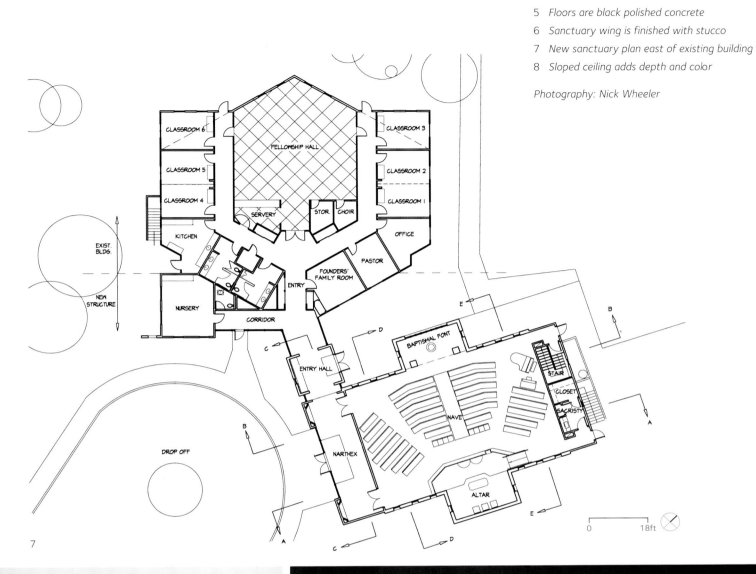

5 Floors are black polished concrete
6 Sanctuary wing is finished with stucco
7 New sanctuary plan east of existing building
8 Sloped ceiling adds depth and color

Photography: Nick Wheeler

7

8

First Presbyterian Church of Encino

Abramson Teiger Architects

Located in Encino, California, this renovation began with a 1954 typical A-frame church with tapering glulam columns and a stone exterior. The project goals were to provide a higher quality of illumination; to develop a form that would promote a greater sense of closeness and transcendence; and to use the dynamic, transformative character of light to heighten the sense of the ecstatic, of being brought into the revelation of divine grace and wisdom.

The pews were arranged to cluster around the altar, while the chancel floor was brought forward and lowered to bring the pastor and choir closer to the congregation. Light as a metaphor of divine presence and spiritual revelation is the primary symbol and theme for this new design.

Light is shaped in three movements that take one on a procession of enlightenment. The first movement represents entering the house of God. The light in the narthex filters from above; its source is not evident. There is a suggestion of a space beyond, yet the main sanctuary remains mysterious.

The second movement corresponds to the main worship space. The interior is illuminated by large openings to the north, which fill the sanctuary with tender light representative of God's love and charity. Light sources to the south are low, creating a common horizon of more brilliant light inside.

The third movement is the most brilliant and varied. Only here does light flow directly down the curved surfaces that shape the sanctuary, illuminating the full form of the church. A multiplicity of openings creates a symphony of light that continually changes the illumination of the cross and place of communion.

The greatest challenge was to create a space in which the curved panels flanking the aisle vary from side to side, making the perspective view subservient to the larger issues of changing light, temporal light, and the ecclesiastical procession towards the chancel. The presence of the cross symbolically rises to become the highest focal point.

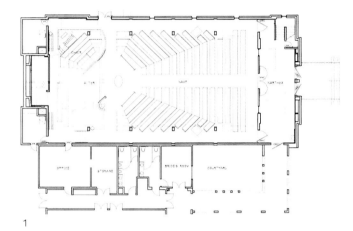

1

2

1 Renovated sanctuary plan

2 Glimpse of sanctuary from narthex

Opposite

   New plaster surfaces modulate light

Photography: Abraham Teiger Architects

Padre Pio Pilgrimage Church

Renzo Piano Building Workshop

San Giovanni Rotondo is one of the most visited pilgrimage destinations in Italy. Each year hundreds of thousands of pilgrims gather here to visit the place where Padre Pio, the friar famous for his stigmata, once lived, and to pay him homage.

To accommodate the ever-increasing number of pilgrims, the monks decided to build a larger, welcoming place of worship not far from the site where the existing church and monastery are located. The major challenge for such a building was to create a space that would be open and inviting. Rather than intimidate the followers, it had to incite a desire in them to draw closer. The immense but low-lying dome provides a sheltering space.

From above, the structure appears spiral shaped, converging at a central dome. When approached from ground level, the building reaches its highest point at the edge overhanging the square. Here the dome tapers slightly, as if bidding visitors welcome. Nearly 6500 can be seated inside the place of worship itself, while 30,000 people can take part in religious services from the piazza outside.

To maintain the sense of welcome, the paving on the square extends into the church, integrating the inside and the outside of the structure, and making it into a kind of "open house." The dome is supported by 22 arches of a mountain stone known as Bronzetto, a local marble that comes from the quarries near Apricena. The largest arch is 16 meters high and 50 meters long. Centuries after being used as the main structural element in Gothic cathedrals, this material is now being employed in new ways, drawing on advanced technology (computerized structural designs, laser-based cross-sectional images, etc.). In addition to this ancient material, others include stainless steel V-struts (for supports between the arches and the roof), laminated larch timber for the upper beams, and pre-oxidized copper for the roof finishing.

1

2

1   Sheltering roof shells hover over each other
2   Roofing material has pre-oxidized patina
3   Sanctuary level plan
4   More than 20 stone arches support the roof
5   Natural light penetrates roof shell voids

Photography: Gianni Berengo Gardin

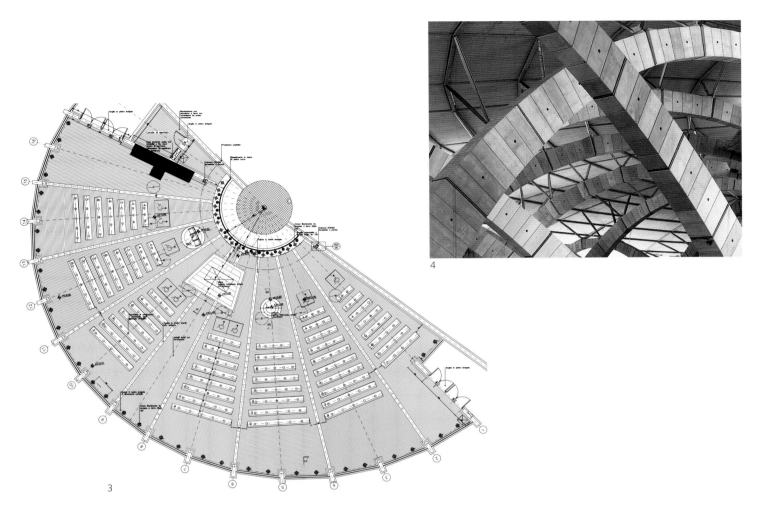

3

4

5

First Church of Christ, Scientist

Rodman Paul and Tarek Ashkar

The congregation of the First Church of Christ, Scientist, Flushing, New York, owned an early-20th century Federalist-style church, which became too costly to maintain. The church sold that property and dedicated the proceeds to building a new house of worship. The challenge was to design a new facility consistent with the congregation's mission, vision, and available resources. According to the architects, Rodman Paul and Tarek Ashkar, the congregation's desire for a conceptually pure sanctuary space was clearly expressed, and it offered continuous encouragement during the design process. The budgetary restraints were accepted as a given, but were not used to limit the ideas under consideration.

The site selected by the congregation is in a residential neighborhood of mixed density. Older single-family houses are interspersed with brick apartment buildings and a great number of churches, temples, and mosques. The congregation wanted a building with a contemporary identity and character, but it also requested that the new structure be contextually sensitive. For the most part, the exterior is clad with a low-cost stucco. The street elevations, composed with plum ironspot brick and olive green stucco, have been welcomed with enthusiasm by the congregation as well as the local community. The brickwork is used sparingly, and the central lobby and gathering space is clad with off-the-shelf curtain-wall glazing.

The new facility includes a sanctuary, administrative offices with a meeting area, and a public reading room. The sanctuary, modern and serene, provides a contemplative environment for worship. A screen-wall dominates the room with an abstract composition of openings. Its reverse side is painted a warm yellow, and reflected light from concealed windows casts a golden glow over the entire sanctuary. The rectangular shapes of the screen wall are repeated in the pattern of the ceiling, with skylights providing a balancing light of a different hue.

2

Opposite

Brick and stucco are predominant materials

2 *Sanctuary uses reflected colored light*

FIRST CHURCH OF CHRIST, SCIENTIST
OF FLUSHING, NY

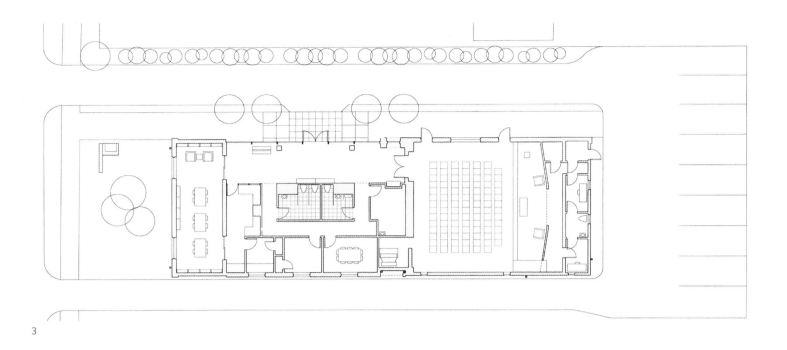

3

4

5

3   Sanctuary level plan

4   Reading room located near entry

5   Glazed entry with reading room beyond

Opposite

  White lobby leads to sanctuary

Photography: Catherine Tighe

Beth Am Israel Synagogue

Voith & Mactavish Architects

The congregation of Beth Am Israel in Penn Valley, Pennsylvania, sought a space that would deepen its ancient faith and enrich its contemporary community. Through a collaborative process, the architects developed a plan that makes optimum use of an ecologically challenging sloped site and a demanding program for a new 25,000-square-foot worship center. The existing 1970's building was demolished and replaced by a new synagogue that features a two-story main sanctuary space surrounded by 11 classrooms, a small chapel, and a social hall for non-religious events and social gatherings.

The synagogue has two entrances: the lower is for everyday access, the upper is open only when the sanctuary is in use. A welcoming portico encourages informal fellowship among community members. Once inside, a vestibule separates the lobby from the sanctuary, which is flanked by galleries on two levels. Collectively, these spaces are the transition zones between *kodesh* and *chol*, between the sacred and the everyday.

As the congregation's central function is Shabbat prayer and learning, the sanctuary is at the heart of the building. Centered and yet directional, the sanctuary conveys seriousness of purpose through proportion, harmony, and order. Tall windows illuminate the space with natural light and frame dramatic views of the surrounding wooded landscape, while custom lighting fixtures are suspended from an exposed wooden truss system. Located directly above the ark, the *ner tamid*, or eternal light, is topped by a hexagonal window inscribed with the Star of David. Framed with Jerusalem stone, the ark is the focal centerpiece of the space and represents the Jewish belief in the Word that illuminates the path through life.

Reflecting the Jewish belief that worship and learning are inseparable parts of a larger whole, classrooms encircle the sanctuary. This arrangement has a practical purpose: During normal Shabbat services (80–100 people), the articulating walls between the classrooms and the sanctuary remain in place. During the High Holidays, when attendance reaches 600, these walls can be quickly moved to expand the sanctuary. Such flexibility allows services to feel both intimate and monumental.

1

1 *Ark is surmounted by the eternal light*
2 *Building section*
3 *Upper-level entrance used during worship*

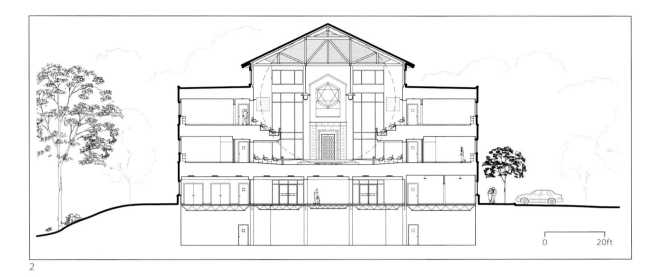

2

3

4

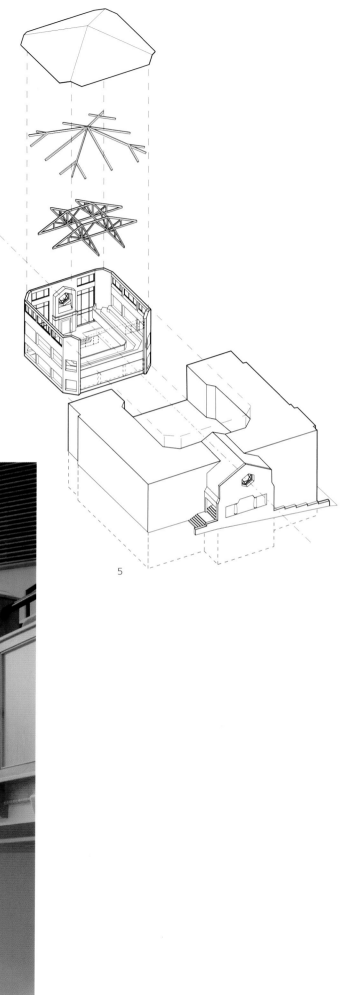

5

6

4   *Detail of balcony rail*
5   *Diagram of synagogue's sanctuary location*
6   *Rendering of sanctuary space*
7   *Sanctuary level plan*
Following pages
   Interior is filled with light and views

Photography: Tom Bernard

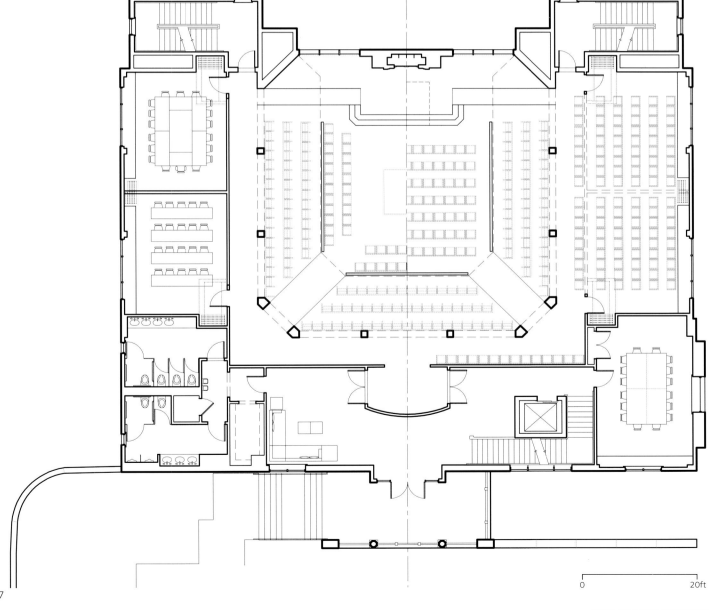

7

Dominican Chapel of Our Lady of the Rosary

Martin Holub Architects & Planners

This program for this new chapel in Sparkill, New York, included a worship space with flexible seating accommodating up to 300 but one that should feel intimate with half as many; easy access for frail and infirm elderly sisters living in the infirmary on the second floor of the existing motherhouse; a small Eucharistic chapel suitable for quiet prayer and contemplation; a gathering space for social contact before and after liturgy both indoors and out; a reconciliation room; a vesting sacristy; a work sacristy; and music storage.

Overall, the guiding principle of the design was the motto "God does not waste a gesture." No effort was spared in paring the design down to the essentials. Another design objective was for the chapel to be an integral part of the existing convent's compound, while at the same time to become its spiritual fulcrum. This is achieved by using materials found in the existing motherhouse, but in a strikingly different form.

With a plan of an irregular hexagon, the two-story chapel is attached to the existing motherhouse on the first and second of its three floors. A bridge over the gathering space below links the chapel's balcony with the convent's infirmary, providing direct access for the sisters living there. The balcony, surrounding the entire chapel, provides space for single rows of wheelchairs and armchairs. A glass railing allows unobstructed views of the worship space below, fostering a sense of unity among all members of the community. The seating layout accommodates both large and small gatherings.

The Eucharistic chapel occupies a distinct space in the easternmost part of the main chapel and is in one's direct line of vision upon entering it. It is separated from the main worship space by the second floor balcony bridge that, together with the different ceiling treatment, gives it the sense of a separate entity. The Eucharistic chapel is also clearly expressed on the exterior.

1

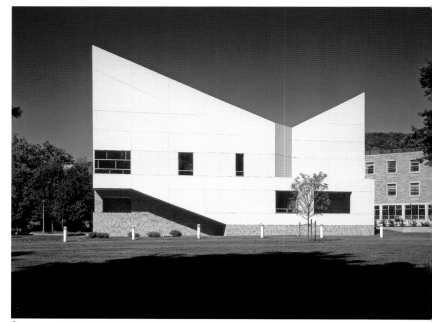

2

1 Chapel's dynamic forms are elegant yet spare
2 Materials echo those of the motherhouse beyond
3 Light materials and finishes distinguish interior
4 Open stair leads to balcony seating
5 Upper level connects directly to infirmary

Photography: Peter Paige

3

4

5

Northeastern University Multi-Faith Spiritual Center

Office dA

The Northeastern University Multi-Faith Spiritual Center is a unique institution on the university's Boston campus that provides a common space where the people of different spiritual, religious, and cultural orientations may come together under one roof for prayer, reflection, and constructive dialogue. This differs from conventional university halls of prayer, which are conceived as non-denominational chapels—sacred spaces for no specific religion. The challenge of the design was to provide for the specific requirements of distinct religious faiths while simultaneously maintaining the necessary neutrality so as not to bias any specific orientation, faith, or iconography.

The Center's two antechambers function as mediators and collector spaces for the various user groups. The east antechamber is a meeting room and small library, which also contains generous storage units for religious and ceremonial artifacts. To the west, the other antechamber houses a foot-wash used for ablution, and storage of shoes and carpets. Both of these rooms are deemed secular in nature, so that artifacts of divergent and sometimes contradictory nature may coexist without being sacrilegious.

Nestled between the antechambers is the main hall—a sacred space where large and small groups alike may come together for everyday events, ceremonies, or formal functions. Given the specific requirements of each user group, the features of the sacred space are designed to accommodate a variety of functions. The space is clad in glass illuminated from behind in order to create an ethereal ambiance for the services; multiple lighting settings allow one to "tune" the space to different moods depending on the nature of the event. Oriented on an east-west axis, the space is capped with three suspended domes that establish three foci for the room. Along the same lines, movable seating and carpets can be arranged to reinforce the lighting schemes and provide for the variety of events that take place in the space.

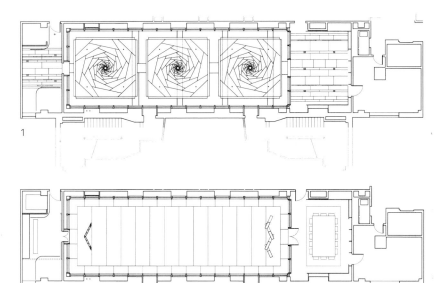

1

2

3

1   *Reflected ceiling plan*
2   *Worship level plan*
3   *One of worship space's three focal domes*
4   *Space fitted with prayer carpets*
5   *Movable seating supports flexibility*
6   *Glass panels are illuminated from behind*
7   *Antechambers connect with worship space*

Photography: Dann Bibb

4

5

6

7

Church of the Resurrection

DiLoreto Architecture

odern Roman Catholic liturgy and this congregation's desire to make a place with a strong sense of community are the key influences that shaped the design of this church in Tualatin, Oregon. Through a series of town hall programming workshops, the congregation articulated its need for an 800-seat church sited to take advantage of the distant northern views, filled with natural light, easily accessible to existing structures, and constructed of local materials. Beyond fulfilling liturgical requirements, the church also had to respond to the parishioners' desire for a place that was communal and uplifting.

The new church is placed on its sloping site to provide easy access between it and existing structures. The placement forms an outdoor courtyard that becomes a gathering place for people before and after services. A generous stairway leads from the parking turn-around to the courtyard and ramps from both upper and lower parking areas make the place fully accessible.

While contemporary in appearance, the building's form responds to its interior spaces. The west entry, side aisles, large vertical windows, and curved apse wall recall traditional church elements, while the exterior brick and cedar board-and-batten connects the building to a Northwest building tradition.

Inside, the entry narthex, immersion baptismal font, center and side aisles, and altar/sanctuary space are arranged to accommodate Catholic liturgical rites. The pews are placed in a half-circle around the raised sanctuary to allow the worshipers to see each other and be closer to the altar. Two 80-foot-long concrete beams provide a column-free interior. The naturally finished douglas fir ceiling rises asymmetrically from the entry in three directions to provide windows along the north and south, bringing in views and natural light. The ceiling reaches its highest point over the altar, emphasizing its importance. The ceiling contrasts with the symmetrical pew layout and is an attempt to symbolize the resurrection. Materials such as concrete, wood, plaster, and bronze are naturally finished.

1

2

1 West entry leads directly to sanctuary
2 Exterior materials relate to local building tradition
3 Sanctuary level plan
4 Daily chapel is adjacent to sanctuary altar
5 Sanctuary roofs rise toward altar area

Photography: Peter Eckert

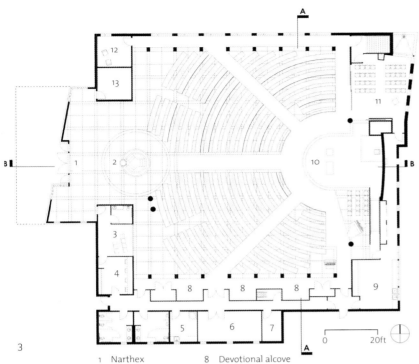

3

1	Narthex	8	Devotional alcove
2	Baptismal font	9	Sacristy
3	Quiet room	10	Sanctuary
4	Changing room	11	Day chapel
5	Janitor room	12	Reconciliation chapel
6	Storage	13	Multipurpose
7	Electrical room		

4

5

Congregation Rodeph Sholom Chapel

Pasanella + Klein Stolzman + Berg Architects

Congregation Rodeph Sholom occupies a synagogue on New York City's Upper West Side that was completed in 1930. The original building is known for its beautiful mix of Moorish, Gothic, and Byzantine Revival styles. The interior space is simple and austere, reflecting the formal manner in which its congregation held services at the time of its construction.

As the congregation expanded over the years, its members desired a smaller, spiritual environment to supplement the main sanctuary and allow worshippers to interact with one another and be involved more directly in the liturgy—a new rooftop chapel.

Due to the synagogue's location in an historic district, local regulations required that the chapel be concealed from the street. The addition is set back from the street to hide it from view. This configuration creates an outdoor courtyard next to the chapel. The chapel's indoor and outdoor spaces are joined by a continuous line of windows that form the exterior wall of the addition.

The chapel's interior is a refined, modern style with traditional religious elements that refer to the spirit and practice of the Jewish liturgy. A high, curved wall separates the spiritual space from the corridor. The color and expanse of the wall make a subtle reference to the Wailing Wall, considered by Jews to be a sacred place. Exterior columns feature Jerusalem stone from Israel.

The new chapel has flexible seating surrounding the reading table, which is placed at the same level as the seating, making the services more accessible to congregants. Moveable partitions to the rear of the chapel allow the space to expand into the adjacent multipurpose room for High Holidays or special religious events. The ark is moved to the center of the chapel when the room is extended so that it remains close to all participants.

Both the chapel and the social hall open to the new roof garden. With city and park views, the terrace provides a unique outdoor space for religious and life-cycle celebrations.

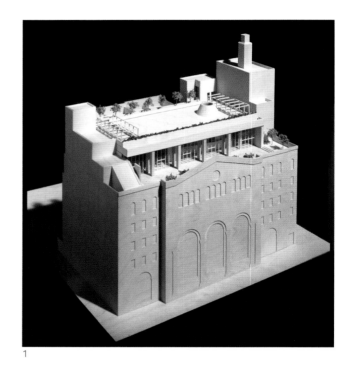

1

1 Model of new rooftop worship space
2 Plan arranged for High Holidays
3 Plan arranged for smaller worship group
4 Synagogue's 1930-era Moorish sanctuary

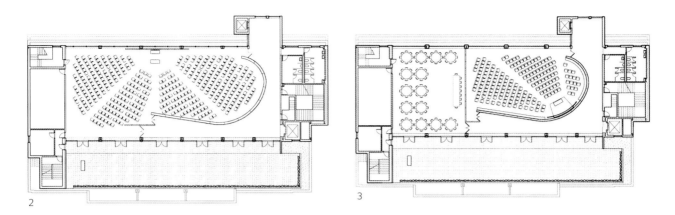

2

3

4

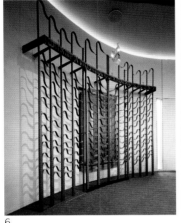

6

7

5   *Rooftop lobby leads to new sanctuary*
6   *Ark with gates closed*
7   *Gates open for access to Torah scrolls*
8   *Wall materials allude to Wailing Wall*
9   *Ark location for smaller worship group*

Photography: Paul Warchol

8

9

First United Methodist Church

Gould Evans

The growing congregation for this church in Blue Springs, Missouri, acquired a 22-acre farmstead near Lake Tapawingo for its new facilities. Using a consensus-building process based on a series of "town hall" meetings, a dramatic and realistic concept for the master plan was developed. The masterplan for the site articulates a strong interplay between the natural features of the rolling site and the desire for an inspiring, sacred awareness in form.

The program calls for a 550-seat sanctuary, music rehearsal space, child development spaces, and classrooms. This building is the first of several phases. In the future this worship space will serve as the narthex and fellowship hall for a much larger sanctuary.

The sanctuary is set back from the street, located on the highest point of the site, with large windows to the east serving as a beacon at night. The building will expand into a village of structures stepping down the hill, framing a central courtyard. A simple rock and water baptismal font is placed beneath an east-facing window on axis with a pond to the west. The sanctuary opens to the west with views of the landscape and the pond. Classrooms and narthex spaces flank the sanctuary and create an outdoor worship space.

The entrance to the narthex lobby is a semi-circular masonry arc, a focal point for worshippers. The sanctuary is a simple shed form that rises to the east. The western edge of the sanctuary is a pedestrian-scaled colonnade with floor-to-ceiling glass providing views of the worship gardens and the worship trail. The east edge of the sanctuary has a continuous band of clerestory glass, shaded with vertical wood louvers and controlled with a deep interior soffit to wash light along the inside wall.

The ceiling graduates in height towards a primary vault above the chancel. Three wood-wrapped bays opening to the south allow traces of light to move across the floor towards the chancel. These three openings are placeholders for the future access to the ultimate, permanent worship space.

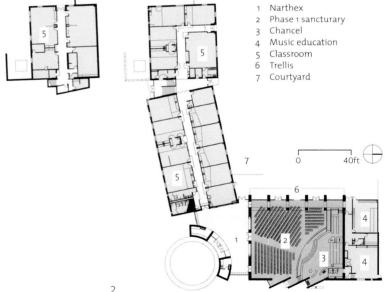

1

1 Narthex
2 Phase 1 sancturary
3 Chancel
4 Music education
5 Classroom
6 Trellis
7 Courtyard

0   40ft

7

2

3

4

1 Altar and reredos in corner of chancel

2 Floor plan

3 Curved wall welcomes worshippers

4 East wall becomes a beacon at night

Photography: Michael Sinclair

Kate and Laurence Eustis Chapel

Eskew+Dumez+Ripple

This small chapel was commissioned by the Ochsner Clinic Foundation in New Orleans, Louisiana, to serve the spiritual needs of the hospital's patients and their families, visitors, and staff. The design of this interdenominational chapel could not rely on specific religious symbols or iconography to assert its claim as sacred space. Instead, the design employs more universal themes of healing and reconciliation to engage visitors with the spiritual.

Seen from the hospital corridor, the chapel manifests a mysterious, luminous presence. A high window provides a partial view to an enigmatic wood scrim. The darkened entry vestibule begins to establish a ritualistic sequence of spaces that anticipate a place of prayer. Light emanates from within the chapel through a wood-framed stained-glass wall narrowing to an entry door. The vestibule's ebony-stained oak floor gradually ramps up to the glass entry door.

The chapel has three distinct spaces: a main worship space (seating a maximum of 12) along with two smaller rooms for private meditation. Upon entering the main space one is transported from the institutional hospital environment to a personally reflective realm. The calming sound of water is immediately apparent. A woven wood ceiling envelops and defines the main seating area. Seemingly untethered and floating within the room, this wooden "shroud" hovers over visitors like a luminescent curtain, providing tactile warmth and symbolic shelter.

Daylight spills into the space from a concealed window near a fountain source, illuminating a channel of water that washes the interior surface of the wall before dropping into a basin beneath a set of cast-glass tablets. Lit from below, the glowing glass shelf is a repository for personal artifacts and mementos visitors might bring to the space while praying. Cherry furnishings (pews, bench, and a movable podium) help define the space.

Two adjacent rooms are for more intimate meditation and prayer. Each has a window for natural light and as a focus for reflection. Cherry plywood wainscoting rises six feet, where a continuous light strip washes the wall with an ethereal glow.

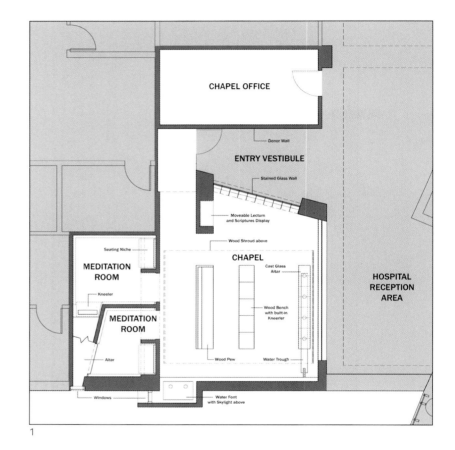

1

1 *Chapel level plan*
2 *Entry vestibule to chapel*
3 *Worship space seating faces wooden "shroud"*
4 *Essential elements of wood, glass, and water*

Photography: Timothy Hursley

2

3

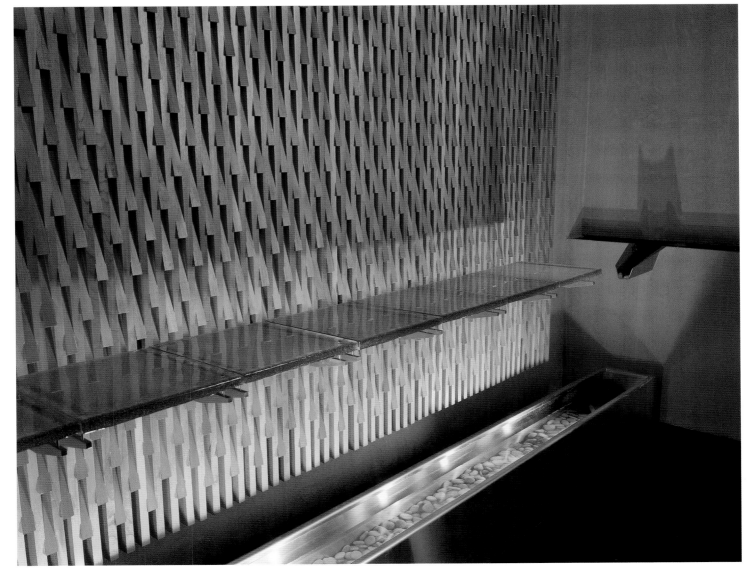

4

Congregation Beth Israel

The Office of Michael Rosenfeld

The synagogue for Congregation Beth Israel in North Adams, Massachusetts, embodies many key religious archetypes that most people recognize—pillar, tree, stone, sacred mountain, among them. By virtue of the integration of the building with its site, as well as the use of custom movable partitions, it creates an atmosphere that is at once intimate and awesome. With the ark as the focus and key structural element of the building, the synagogue is an authentic manifestation of the core value of the congregation–community built on The Word.

The building is fully integrated into its surroundings, curving and undulating in response to the surrounding hills, closing and sheltering from residential neighbors and north winds, opening to the magnificent views to the south and west. Trees and roof overhangs create shade and sun control in the summer while site placement and plan organization maximize daylight and desirable solar heat gain in winter. Thermal strategies minimize heat loss and control heat gain for the highly diverse occupancy and uses of the building.

Visitors encounter a low entry that gives way to a soaring, high-ceilinged sanctuary. Light streams through high windows while a glass façade admits surrounding mountain vistas. Only the ark, which serves as both the spiritual and structural center of the building, interrupts this expanse of glass in order to support the roof and form the focal point within the sanctuary.

The custom-designed moveable partitions provide flexibility. The congregation wanted something more dignified than the typical institutional partitions. The architect worked closely with a manufacturer to create a beautiful solution appropriate to the sacredness of the space. The curved tracking follows the lines of the building. The partitions are used to form a library, social hall, and small sanctuary. When the partitions are open, the space becomes one large sanctuary that can accommodate 230 people during the High Holidays, or a social hall that can hold 150 tables for a banquet.

1

2

1   *Synagogue with hills in the distance*
2   *Natural materials greet visitors at entry*
3   *Partitions in place create intimate space*
4   *Partitions removed for larger gatherings*

Photography: Robert Benson

3

4

House of Prayer Oratory

Cuningham Group Architecture

Resting on five acres of woodland alongside a retreat center at Saint John's Abbey in Collegeville, Minnesota, this intimate building is designed as an oasis for peaceful meditation and personal reflection for visitors seeking a rejuvenation of spirit and faith through prayer.

To reach the Oratory, one walks 50 feet on a simple boardwalk leading from the retreat center. The walk is a metaphor for embarking on a spiritual journey and can be considered a commitment of faith during a typical Northern Minnesota winter. Conceived as a gabled "little building in the woods," the interior surprises visitors with rounded, 16-sided walls of honey-colored Baltic birch. The multi-layered, wooden ceiling is evocative of the tents in which the tribes of Israel took shelter.

Up to 24 people can gather in the 1000-square-foot, meticulously crafted space. Wood materials create a warm and welcoming atmosphere, while fabrics provide a soft, tactile experience. Grounding the space in nature, a clerestory window at the ceiling's peak sits directly over a 48-inch circle of exposed earth, rimmed by Minnesota granite. The relationship of the window and bare earth suggests the connection between heaven and earth, imbuing the building with a sense of both the immanent and the transcendent. A diamond-shaped window provides a glimpse of the context, the forest beyond. Smaller windows in the alcoves capture natural light changes through the day, while indirect lighting gently illuminates the space at night. Although the floor plan resembles the shape of a Celtic cross, traditional Christian icons are minimal and removable, in keeping with the Oratory's ecumenical nature.

The Oratory also serves as a physical statement of the importance of uncovering the art of listening. A primary design challenge was to preserve the richness of silence experienced in the building's woodland setting. This is reflected in a number of design decisions; specifically, the choice of radiant heat in lieu of a noisier forced-air system. Special consideration was given to providing extraordinary sound control. The interior is designed to maximize the acoustics of the human voice. When voices are raised in prayer, the acoustics are exceptionally pleasing.

1

0   12ft

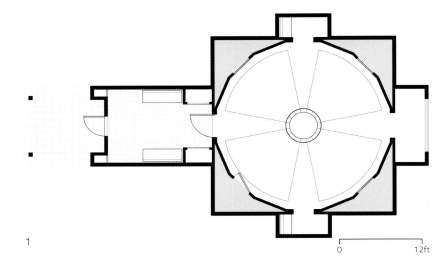

2

1 *Entry level plan*
2 *The building is a retreat in the woods*
3 *Views from diamond-shaped windows*
4 *Tent-like ceiling draws eyes upward*
Opposite
   Circle of earth connects with heaven

Photography: Christian Korab

3

4

First Unitarian Church of St. Louis

Powers Bowersox Associates

Originally designed by the noted St. Louis architect William B. Ittner, this small, picturesque stone building was built in 1917. The first addition was an educational classroom wing, built in 1960, with buff-colored brick chosen to harmonize with the warm gray stone of the original church. Later, the congregation built a memorial garden adjacent to the sanctuary and the educational wing. The current congregation wished to add a 100-seat multipurpose chapel. The architects chose a small parking lot on the open side of the memorial garden, facing a prominent city street. The placement of the chapel provides a new public image, visual connections to several neighboring churches, and the opportunity to create a more private space for the memorial garden.

The chapel and garden work together as an indoor and outdoor space. The chapel was designed as a flexible seating space whose primary visual orientation is toward the memorial garden and the 1917 stone sanctuary. A transparent wall contains 11 doors that open directly into the garden, and engages the user with both the garden and the church. The geometry of the room consists of simple shapes, while variety is achieved through volumetric forms, light and shade, and light quality that changes throughout the day. A stained-glass window saved from the congregation's earliest church is placed in one of the walls as an historical focal point. The floating ceiling lends a sense of shelter as well as diffusing sunlight from the clerestory windows. Previously, services were not held during the summer due to the intense heat—now a quiet new air-conditioning system makes it possible. The chancel was extended to accommodate additional choir seating. A new bay window/children's seating area was created for the nursery in the education wing whose window was lost with the new chapel addition.

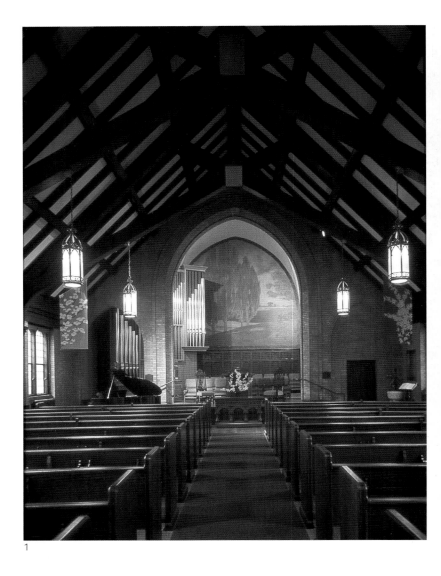

1

1   *Original 1917 stone sanctuary*
2   *Detail of new chapel's stone and copper exterior*
3   *Doors open out to garden from chapel*
4   *Stonework echoes original building*

2

3

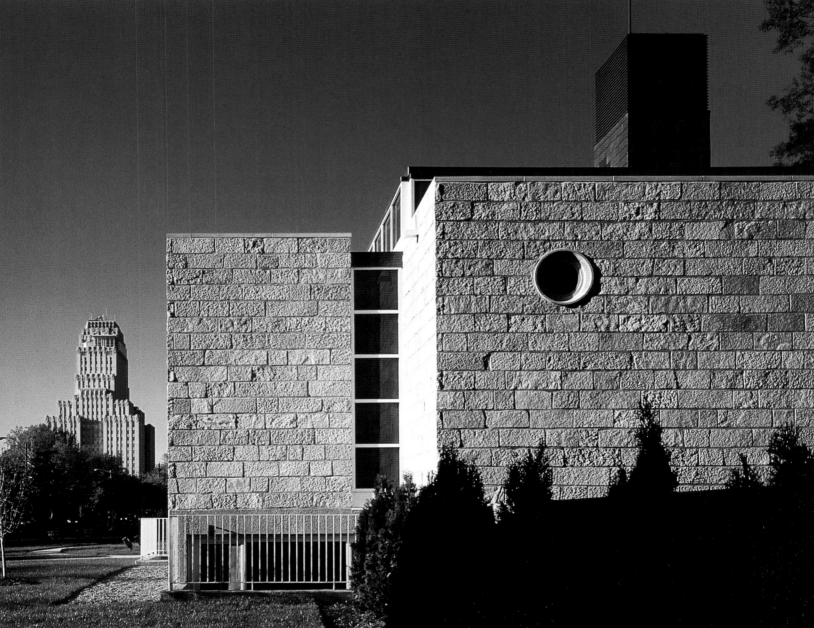

4

5

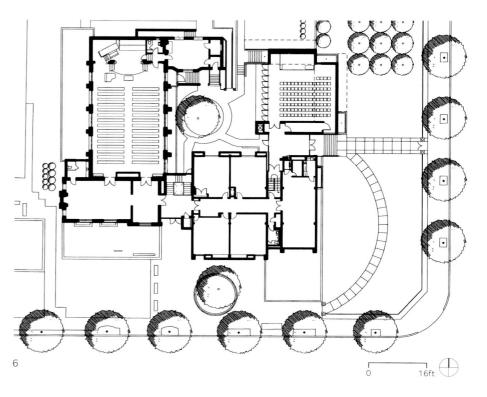

6

7

0   16ft

8

9

5   Interior light is balanced
6   Ground level plan
7   Chapel ceiling appears to float
8   Simple materials crisply detailed
9   Refurbished lounge space
10   Narthex leads to garden or chapel

Photography: Robert Pettus

10

Overlake Park Presbyterian Church

Olson Sundberg Kundig Allen Architects

This new worship space replaces a previous sanctuary that was destroyed by fire. The design of the new sanctuary is purposely abstract and meant to inspire contemplation, as well as serve as the focal point for this church campus in Bellevue, Washington. The addition of a new narthex provides a quiet transition between the existing church and the new sanctuary.

The design reinforces contemplation by using a limited material palette to create a simple space that relies on the naturally ethereal qualities of light to support the desired worship experience. The stucco exterior gives the church an abstract quality in pure white, heightening the mystery of the church. Light, both natural and artificial, shapes the church's interior. Rectangular in plan, a central clerestory running the length of the nave up to the chancel diffuses light throughout the space. A saw-tooth side wall along the north façade creates interior drama by introducing direct sunlight while limiting views to the exterior, and reinforcing the abstract quality of the interior.

The chancel is accentuated by an even wash of light along its curved back wall from a series of concealed windows. The lack of an obvious source for this light reinforces the abstract quality of the sanctuary and gives the surface of the wall an ethereal light that suggests infinity. The pews, font, table, and lectern—all of a simple, elegant design—stand on a single level, reinforcing the unity of all in the space.

1

2

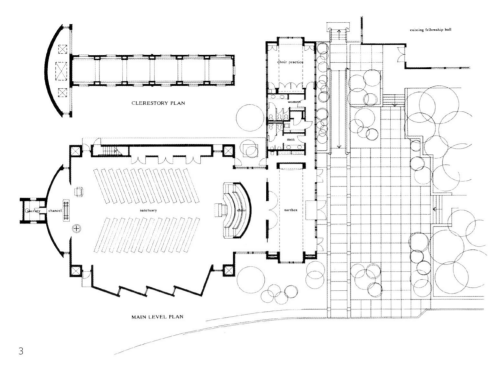

CLERESTORY PLAN

MAIN LEVEL PLAN

3

1 Slanted light of saw-tooth wall
2 Clerestory provides ethereal light
3 Plan with clerestory above
4 White stucco lends abstract appearance

Photography: Robert Pisano

4

Temple Isaiah Renovation

Toshihiko Taketomo Architect
William M. Simmers, Collaborating Architect

With the exception of the laminated wood arches and some exposed structural decking in this renovated 1962 temple in Lexington, Massachusetts, virtually all the finishes in the sanctuary and the chapel are new. Beyond refreshing the surfaces, the intent was to manipulate the sense of envelopment and release in these spaces, through extensive interior design plus the strategic additions of the bema tower, a linear extension along the chapel wing, and a reframed chapel roof with skylight monitor.

The new bema (pulpit and ark platform) and renovated sanctuary celebrate the congregation's sense of unity. The sanctuary is a centrally organized, interactive space achieved by shaping the bema as an extension as much as a culmination of the sanctuary.

Certain qualities of the existing sanctuary are preserved to maintain memories of life-cycle events that have been celebrated there, while transforming it into a brighter, airier, and more uplifting space. The ark-like woodiness and warmth is retained by forming a new interior architecture framed by purlin-like members spanning between the arches and textured acoustical panels custom made from oak slat-work. Transitions of new openness to daylight (enhanced by artificial lighting) fills the space with new life. A framed view of the hillside rises behind the "ark" temple.

Strong simple geometries grow from the hipped roof into the light tower to create a sense of release and ascension to the infinite. This is crowned with a seven-part triangular skylight (echoing the menorah) that presents an emblematic, glowing beacon in the evening and a seemingly endless spatial extension above the bema from the perspective of the sanctuary. A ladder of glass ascends within the tower, opening to the variegated and changing foliage of the hillside beyond.

The new chapel's "in the round" form reflects an egalitarian ethos, within which an ark is reintegrated at one end. The space is filled with natural light, enhanced with controlled artificial light, entirely from above. The space is comfortably intimate for a small minion worship and study group, but also comfortably spacious and airy for a larger gathering of up to 100.

1

1   *Eternal light suspended in tower over ark*
Opposite
    Materials and finishes emphasize openness

3 *Synagogue complex plan*
4 *Light accents chapel detailing*
5 *View from ark of reconfigured space*
6 *Pulpit design echoes architecture*

Photography: John Horner; Toshihiko Taketomo, Architect

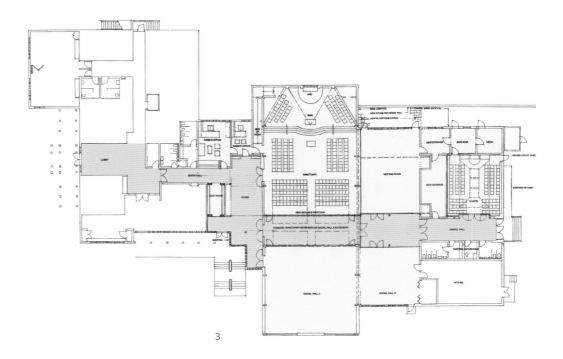

3

4

5

6

William E. Simon Sacred Space

Thompson Naylor Architects

This small sacred space for the Cottage Hospital in Santa Barbara, California, was designed to be a peaceful oasis within a tense and busy hospital and a place to aid the healing process. The size, scale, and configuration of the space are intended to be versatile: comfortable for one person in silent meditation, or for services for up to 40 people.

The sacred space announces itself in the hospital corridor with elliptical windows and a "river of life" glass door (adapted from Spanish mission doors), permitting glimpses into the vestibule. The vestibule is a transition from the hectic world of the hospital to the tranquil world that the chapel offers. Its illuminated niches along a wall house a rotating collection of religious objects donated by local faith groups.

The chapel itself is a more universally nondenominational spiritual space, leaving behind the religious symbols of the vestibule. It capitalizes on its rooftop location with a soaring glass wall under a shell-like roof. At the glass wall is a raised platform that helps to define the interior space, while still allowing views out. When seated, one's eye level follows the surface of the roofscape. At the opposite end of the glass wall, a concealed skylight washes a wall with natural light.

The chapel is a simple, timeless form that is finished with natural materials: hand-troweled plaster walls, wood ceiling, rough stone tops, and natural wool carpeting. These materials extend through the glass wall to allow the chapel to visually include the outdoor space beyond.

1

1 *Rooftop chapel with shell-like form*
2 *Large window wall opens the space*
3 *Illuminated niche displays objects*
4 *Entry features "river of life" glass door*
5 *Chapel shape defines focus*

Photography: Glenn E. Dubock

3

4

2

5

Komyo-Ji Temple

Tadao Ando Architect & Associates

A reconstruction of a Pure land temple dating from the Edo period, this project is on the eastern side of the small city of Saijo in the Ehime Prefecture. About 250 years had passed since the construction of the main temple and it was no longer able to withstand the assaults of time. It was to be rebuilt, together with the adjoining guest hall and priests' quarters. The chief priest desired "a temple where people will come to gather together, a temple that is open to the community."

Ando's elegant solution is a building of wood, shrouded in gentle light and floating over a spring-fed pond. This arrangement stresses water and wood as the essential features of the local landscape. The main theme was an exploration of space in wood. While there is no preoccupation with the existing temple's architecture, there is a desire to respect what has been built up through history.

Ando explains that, to him, the essence of traditional Japanese wooden architecture is "assembly." A great number of wooden parts are cut for a single building, which takes shape as these parts are assembled. Ando wanted to create a building that would return to the origins of wooden architecture, a single structure made up of multiple parts, each full of tension. The building's framework would express the image of people gathering and joining hands, supporting each other in a single community.

Three layers of interlocking beams of laminated timber are supported by 16 columns in four groups. The periphery of the temple is a screen of frosted glass, then a corridor around the screen, and then a latticed exterior wall around the corridor. Light filters through the lattice wall to fill the interior with soft, natural illumination. At night, the mystical appearance of the main building, with light overflowing from the interior, is reflected in the water's darkness. Every attempt was made to leave stone walls and vegetation around the site undisturbed.

Water and wood, history and landscape, the temple becomes a place where a variety of elements come together and speak to the visitor.

1   Temple's inner sanctum
2   Elevation/site section

1

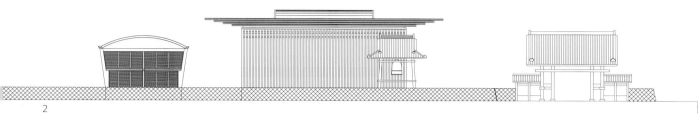

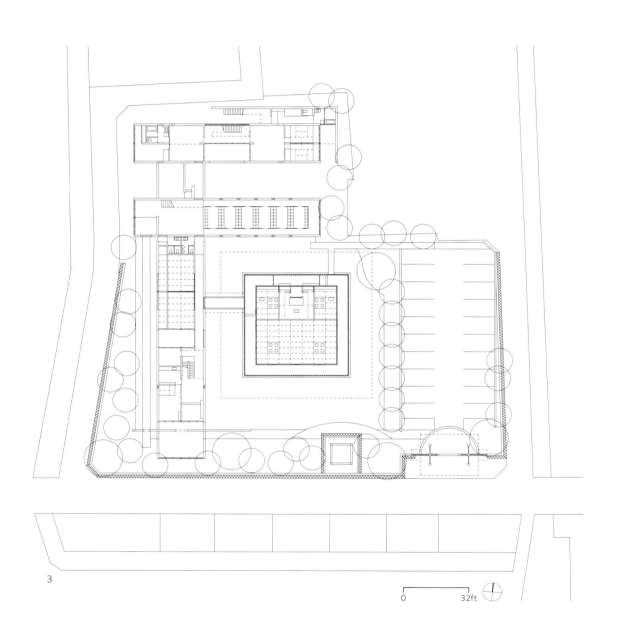

3

0   32ft

4

3   Temple level plan

4   Building reflected in spring-fed pond

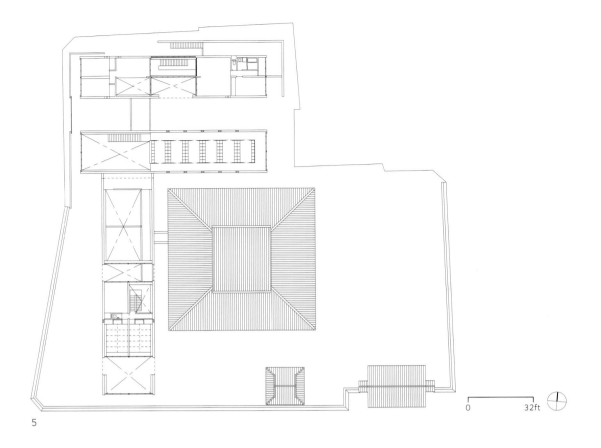

5

0   32ft

6

5 Roof plan
6 Glass screens' reflection/transparency
7 Wood screen corridor around temple
8 Detail of glass and wood temple enclosure

Photography: Mitsuo Matsuoka

7

8

Holy Rosary Catholic Oratory

Trahan Architects

The existing Holy Rosary Church site in Amant, Louisiana, consisted of a modest assemblage of buildings lacking in collective presence and dominated by expanses of landscape. The church community desired an elevated sense of place and spiritual purpose within this powerful natural setting.

The new campus plan unifies parish functions through a coherent organizational system, while drawing a clear distinction between sacred and secular programs. Secular building components take the form of linear "edge" pavilions framing a sacred precinct. Moving clockwise, the courtyard promenade leads to the oratory— the campus focal point.

Predominant in its purity, height, and skewed placement, this 30-foot concrete cube floats within the lawn. The oratory interior is a pure, womb-like space, a 20-foot cubic volume nested and rotated within the larger cube. The reciprocal rotation aligns this sacred space with the main campus, signifying a union of spiritual and secular lives.

The oratory's internal apertures draw light into the space without revealing its source or context. Radiance falls through varied cavities cast into the changing wall thickness of the offset cubes. Openings near the ceiling produce a brilliant glow, while voids near the floor render a soft luminosity. Considering the light symbolically, each aperture is a meditation on an episode of the paschal mystery of Christ.

The passage from the expanse of the courtyard into the intimate oratory chamber is marked by splayed portal walls. The sequence of compression and release is experienced differently as one moves into or out of the oratory. This spatial shift parallels a personal and spiritual transformation taking place. A unique cast-glass door set within the threshold uses light to celebrate this event. Lens-shaped in plan, the door gathers and refracts light, glowing brightly at its edges with a soft luminosity at its middle.

Costly or rare materials are avoided (as is ornamentation) in favor of those expressive of simplicity and permanence. The selected materials posses an abstract nature, elevated through careful treatment and detailing. In this context of striking simplicity, the materials and their relationship with the setting are raised to a poetic level.

1

2

1 *Complex's connected secular buildings*
2 *Secular buildings frame the oratory*
3 *Oratory as mysterious concrete cube*
4 *Solid and glass planes define the campus*
5 *Oratory entry, with pivoted glass door*

3

4

5

6

7

6   Concrete texture under sunlight
7   Illumined oratory as hallowed space
8   Voids in concrete cube admit light

Photography: Timothy Hursley

8

Love of Christ Lutheran Church

Gould Evans

The Love of Christ Lutheran Church in Mesa, Arizona, explores the notion of multipurpose space. The 22,000-square-foot facility program called for a 1000-seat, state-of-the-art contemporary worship space as well as a space for recreational sports and performance.

This unique mix of functions posed many inherent challenges to the design team. The new building needed to respect the scale of existing traditional buildings while satisfying the height requirements of a basketball court. It had to create intimate spaces for worship as well as provide flexible and functional spaces for sports such as basketball. The material palette had to be durable to withstand high impact recreational use, while also having the acoustical and visual appeal for a dignified worship environment.

The design solution reveals these dualities. The overall form takes its cues from the surrounding mountain landscape and reads as a low-rise cluster of solid masses nestled into the desert site. It extends the orthogonal grid of the existing building, unites the existing campus around a new central courtyard, and projects a sense of outreach to the greater community. From the exterior, the building's most identifying feature is a leaning wall that shears across the site like a geologic fault line to split and raise the building's mass towards the street.

The multiuse space is organized around two intersecting axes. The interior of the space parallels the axis of the existing building and is delicately shaped for necessary acoustical reflection and proper sight lines. Major public zones are concealed behind a perforated screen wall with accent lighting that glows at night to attract the attention of passersby. The building merges body and soul together in a response that speaks of its time and place.

1

1 *Detail of brick tower near church entry*
2 *Form echoes contours of nearby hills*
3 *Translucent wall glows as a beacon*
4 *Worship level plan*
5 *Assembly space also used for recreation*

Photography: Bill Timmerman

2

3

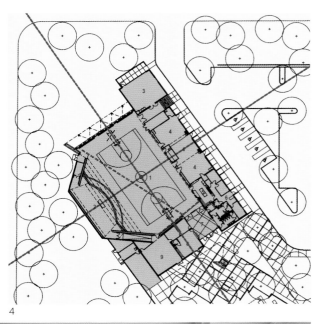

4

5

Antioch Baptist Church

The Rural Studio, Auburn University

Architecture students in Auburn University's Rural Studio, started by the late architect Samuel Mockbee, have been designing and building projects for the poor of rural Alabama since 1993. This project, designed and constructed by students Gabrielle Michaud Fuller, Jared Fulton, Marion McElroy, and Bill Nauck, was instigated by congregation member Cedric Caddell, who said he wanted "the Cadillac of churches." Antioch Baptist's existing church was anything but a Cadillac. Built in 1901, it had a one-room sanctuary, a small vestibule, and a tiny preacher's office. The lack of running water curtailed the congregation's willingness to host the inter-congregational events that are the lifeblood of the rural church community in Perry County, Alabama.

While the students speculated about how to improve the existing facility by adding on to it, the congregation and clergy urged tearing the old church down and starting anew. The building fund was not nearly enough to construct a new church from scratch. The solution was to deconstruct the old building piece-by-piece, saving every scrap of material that could be re-used for a new church. Interior tongue-in-groove cladding was carefully removed, nails were pulled out, and the planks were planed. The timber structure was pulled down and pieces that were free of rot were stored on site for the new construction. Approximately 80 percent of the old church's materials were salvaged for the new building.

The new church is oriented the same way as the old one. The main aisle forms a meaningful central link between the living congregants on one side and the deceased congregants who rest in Antioch's small graveyard on the other, beyond the church's long glass wall. A full-immersion font is found beneath the baptistery, behind the pulpit. When baptismal candidates completely step down into the font, they stand at the same level below grade where rest the congregants in the graveyard, symbolizing that the newly baptized are now ready for death. Where the old church's interior was dark and somber, the new church is filled with natural light, and lined with the wood saved from the old church.

1

1 New church is aligned with graveyard
2 Entry is through narrow end
3 Church is adjacent site of old structure

2

3

4

4 Full-immersion font behind pulpit

5 Interior is lined with recycled planks

6 Roof truss articulates worship space

Photography: Timothy Hursley

5

6

Author's Note

Michael J. Crosbie

Dr Michael J. Crosbie is an internationally recognized author, architect, journalist, critic, and teacher. A former editor of both *Progressive Architecture* and *Architecture* magazines, he is author of more than a dozen books on architecture, including the best-selling first edition of *Architecture for the Gods*, published by The Images Publishing Group in 1999, and *Architecture for the Gods, Book II*, published in 2003. Dr Crosbie has written for a number of journals and magazines, including *Historic Preservation, Domus, Architectural Record, Landscape Architecture,* and *ArchitectureWeek,* and has won several journalism awards. He is the Editor-in-Chief of *Faith & Form* magazine, the interfaith journal of religion, art, and architecture. He lectures widely on religious architecture and design. Dr Crosbie is an adjunct professor at the University of Hartford and at Roger Williams University, and has lectured at architecture schools in North America and abroad. He practices with Steven Winter Associates, an architectural research and consulting firm based in Norwalk, Connecticut.

Acknowledgments

Many people were involved in the creation of this book. Thanks are extended to the architects and designers who agreed to have their projects published (and to the clergy and congregations that had the foresight to build them). Special gratitude is expressed to the photographers who generously allowed use of their photographs. To my colleagues and friends at *Faith & Form* magazine I express my thanks for suggesting projects, architects, artists, and designers. Special thanks are extended to Judith Dupré, Betty Meyer, Julie Taylor, Sandra Vallé, Fr Richard Vosko, and Kenneth Wyner for bringing several projects to my attention. Finally, I wish to thank Alessina Brooks and Paul Latham of The Images Publishing Group, and their staff, especially Aisha Hasanovic, for their support of this publication.